The Synod of Westminster

The Synod of Westminster

DO WE NEED IT?

EDITED BY
Peter Moore

First published in Great Britain 1986
SPCK
Holy Trinity Church
Marylebone Road
London NW1 4DU

British Library Cataloguing in Publication Data
The Synod of Westminster.
1. Church of England. *General Synod*
I. Moore, Peter, *1924*
262'.5342   BX5150

ISBN 0–281–04211–X

Typeset by Latimer Trend & Company Ltd
Crescent Avenue, Plymouth

Printed in Great Britain
at the University Press, Oxford

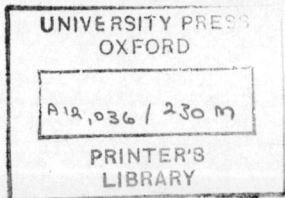

CONTENTS

THE CONTRIBUTORS

PETER MOORE is Dean of St Albans. He has served in parochial ministries in town and country, and was Chaplain of New College, Oxford, and a residentiary canon of Ely. For eight years he was a member of the Church of England Liturgical Commission. He is the author of *Tomorrow is Too Late* and *Footholds in the Faith*, and editor of *Man, Woman, and Priesthood* and *Bishops: But What Kind?*.

ERIC KEMP has been Bishop of Chichester since 1974. From 1941–6 he was Librarian of Pusey House, Oxford, and from 1946–69 Fellow, Chaplain and Tutor of Exeter College, Oxford. He piloted the Synodical Government Measure through the Convocations and the Church Assembly, and in 1969 became Dean of Worcester. He has been Chairman of the Faith and Order Advisory Group since its formation in 1965.

HUGH CRAIG is a Chartered Mechanical Engineer, and Technical Director of an Engineering Company. He has been a member of the House of Laity of the Church Assembly and General Synod continuously since 1950, representing the laity of five dioceses. He served as an elected member of the Standing Committee from 1965 to 1980.

D. W. GUNDRY has been Chancellor of Leicester Cathedral since 1963, and was a member of the General Synod for its first ten years. He was for many years on the staff of the University College of North Wales, Bangor, and later Professor of Religious Studies in the University of Ibadan. He is also Church Affairs correspondent of *The Daily Telegraph* and the author of books on the study of religions.

CLIFFORD LONGLEY has been Religious Affairs correspondent of *The Times* since 1972. He was previously a general reporter, and then assistant news editor and feature writer for the paper. He was commended in the specialist writer section of the British Press Awards 1984. In 1961 he joined the Roman Catholic Church, having previously been an atheist.

ALISTER McGRATH teaches historical theology, ethics and systematic theology at Wycliffe Hall, Oxford, having previously spent several years in parish work in Nottingham. He studied at Oxford, Utrecht and Cambridge, and has the unusual distinction of holding first-class honours degrees from Oxford University in both natural science and theology.

The Contributors

GRAHAM LEONARD has been Bishop of London since 1981. He was consecrated Bishop of Willesden in 1964, and was translated to Truro in 1973. He is Chairman of the General Synod Board of Education, and is the author of several books, the most recent being *Firmly I Believe and Truly*. A Catholic with an Evangelical upbringing, he believes that true radicalism springs from the application of orthodox doctrine.

ENOCH POWELL is Member of Parliament (Ulster Unionist) for South Down, and was for many years the Conservative M.P. for Wolverhampton S.W. A noted scholar and sometime Professor of Greek at Sydney University, he describes himself as 'a "high and dry" Church-and-Queen Anglican, High Tory in politics, historian of the House of Lords and poet'.

GEOFFREY ROWELL has been Fellow, Chaplain and Tutor in Theology at Keble College, Oxford since 1972. He is a Canon of Chichester Cathedral, and since 1980 has been a member of the Liturgical Commission. He has strong ecumenical interests, particularly with the Eastern Churches. His published works include *Hell and the Victorians* and *Vision Glorious*.

1

Synodical Scenario

Peter Moore

It is always easier to demolish than to build, and the contributors to this collection of essays are in no sense destroyers of authority. On the contrary, they are all concerned not only with the nature of authority, but also with the varying ways in which it can be exercised. The visible church must act visibly, in a manner which can be recognized. Sooner or later this means structures, and structures tend as much to limit as to enable. Our main concern has been with those structures, and with one in particular, the General Synod of the Church of England. The high hopes with which it was inaugurated have not been fulfilled. There is disillusionment and frustration, and if that continues there is a real danger of a bitterness which can erode the good. And there is good in the Synod—otherwise we should not spend so much time writing about it, taking part in it, and trying to make it a better servant of the Church.

It is clearly modelled on Parliament, but there are two basic differences which distinguish it from that model.

The first consists in the fact that whereas Parliament is elected on a direct vote of the electorate, the lay members of General Synod are elected, not by a direct vote, but by the deanery synods which have themselves been elected by the total electorate, whereas the clergy are elected by all licensed clergy of the diocese, that is to say their total electorate. Lay members of the Synod therefore are one step removed from what is frequently referred to as the 'grass-roots' level. Quite apart from the constituency of the electorate itself, challenged in these pages most sharply by Mr Powell, whose views seem to coincide with the Lutheran Settlement of Scandinavian churches, the question must be asked whether, and in what sense, the Synod is representative, and representative of whom?

As it stands, it is partly representative of deanery synods which

1

are part of its own infrastructure. And although there were high hopes in 1970 that the new body would be more representative of the wide variety of church members, in age, work and skills, this hope has not been fulfilled, save for the representation of women, who do fare a great deal better in General Synod elections than in national or local government ballots. The use of proportional representation was scouted, examined and rejected in favour of the single transferable vote, and although pressures remain for its use, in Parliament as well as in Synod, the evidence suggests that in fact it tends to paralyse rather than liberate, active government. A glance at the figures produced by Mr Craig in his essay would suggest that, rather than getting better, the Synod is in fact becoming less than ever a reflection of total church life. This will inevitably remain the case if the organization has to meet relatively frequently and for several days at a time, thus effectively disfranchising a very large section of church people. One of the weightiest arguments against the Church Assembly was its unrepresentative nature, for although it was based on a wider electorate, those with time to spare came chiefly from the retired or people of independent means. We heard much of the changes to be brought both at diocesan and national level. The changes, however, are certainly not very obvious, and at least one of the pressing grounds for change has failed.

The second significant difference between Synod and Parliament, and one which strikes at the root of the comparison, consists in the fact that Parliament produces a government which can change—and be changed. No such thing happens in the Synod. Thus there is little motive for hoping for, let alone for working for, any significant change of policy. The Synod has grown greater than the Church Assembly because of its powers; particularly as a result of the Worship and Doctrine Measure which has opened a whole new range of subjects for debate. It has created boards and councils which have to fill agendas and find something to do. Indeed a body largely constituted to deal with questions of doctrine and worship, church order and the relationship of parish and diocese to the centre of the Church spends a disproportionate amount of time on matters covered by paragraph 6 of its constitution 'to consider and express opinions on any other matters of religious or public interest'. It is scarcely surprising that its members tend to regard themselves as a sort of parliamentary scrutineer ready to advise, caution and admonish in a way Parliament scarcely can have envisaged when the Synod was set up in 1970.

The primary function of a parliament, or so it has been at significant moments of our national history, has been to raise money, to keep the government going. It was this very reason that saw both the rise and demise of Convocations. They were revived in the first half of the last century as part of a growing self-awareness of *ecclesia anglicana* in the face of parliamentary religious toleration (and representation). They were also a response to the upheavals of the post-industrial revolution in England. But more than all this, just because they were exclusively clerical assemblies, they spoke with authority on matters of doctrine. That is not to say they were listened to for that reason. But at least they were there and represented a long tradition that the clergy, and especially the bishops, were the guardians of the faith.

The model of parliament has very limited relevance to the conduct of church affairs. Its members are elected on party lines, and that ensures a wide variety of people. They are paid for doing a whole-time job. They can lose the support of their constituency or become leader of their party. They can make—and break—governments. And they are directly accountable to the total electorate who choose them—and they themselves have been chosen by local committees with varying degrees of rigour.

With the exception of accountability by report and re-election, none of these things apply to the Synod, which demands more time than many working people can give, whose polite procedures lack the cut and thrust of debate and whose achievements seem scarcely related to the time they take. Lay members, as distinct from the clergy, are not, in general, elected on a party ticket and in a sense the use of the term *party* is misleading, because it suggests, on the parliamentary comparison, that different parties can achieve alternative government. It is a lamentable fact that the truth of this statement is currently modified by the pressure exerted by the Movement for the Ordination of Women, countered by the Church Union and others. But the episcopal structure of the Church of England rules out the possibility of alternative government.

The cabinet of the Synod is the Standing Committee, and all its procedures are subject to the multiple forces bearing upon it. The influence, for instance, of the Church Commissioners vis-à-vis the Synod is financial; a Treasury influence. And although the First Church Estates Commissioner sits in General Synod by right, he is representing something which is adjacent to and connected with, but not strictly part of, the synodical structure. This complex relationship has effectively baulked any proper debate about the Commissioners on the grounds that they are not part of the synodical system. But their influence upon it and the whole Church cannot be denied.

A wise paragraph in *Government by Synod* (p. 55) notes:

> The keynote of any system of permanent bodies, both at the centre and in the dioceses must ... be service ... In no sense must it be an authoritarian bureaucracy but an organisation with the means to think and study, sensitive to opinion and in touch with the leaders of thought in both Church and state. It must be adequately controlled, yet sufficiently flexible to be capable of rapid adjustment to changing needs.

The power of the permanent civil servants in the Church of England is very considerable and getting more so—and this is bound to be the case as they know what is going on across the whole spectrum of synodical activity. They service committees directly, attend Standing and Policy Committee and accompany members to and from the Legislative committee and are therefore more in command of the facts of the matter than most, or any others, of the Synod. And it is only too easy, for instance, for Standing Committee to accept a statement as one of fact rather than of bureaucratic opinion. Considerable influence rests with someone quick and administratively competent who is servicing a committee at sixes and sevens amongst themselves. 'It is not the custom to do this or that', should perhaps be more often countered with the assertion, 'Then it's high time we started.' Decisions are made by the responsible committee, but very often in the light of information or comment which is fed in, and which make it far more reasonable to accept one thing rather than another. A current example of this has been the Standing Committee's reversed decision concerning Article 7 business on the Deaconess' measure on advice from one of its own bureaucrats.

It is here that a distinction of functions needs to be made. Matters which are primarily administrative need to be dealt with

4

differently from those which are pastoral, liturgical and doctrinal. Yet how seldom does the Synod have the time—or apparently the desire—for theological debate? One reason of course is that it is not equipped for this, any more than it is for the consideration of complex problems such as unemployment, on which it is far from backward on making superficial pronouncements. Indeed a proliferation of its own activities has encouraged the Synod to think that unless it has pronounced on some matter of moment, the Church has not spoken. The laws, not of the Medes and Persians, but of Parkinson and Peters have established themselves. The Board of Social Responsibility, for instance, created to work out the existing social responsibilities of the Church like adoption societies and moral welfare, now engages in discussing matters of international importance like the bomb, apartheid and housing associations and a whole gamut of things with which, because of its wide terms of reference, it can occupy itself. Parliament, however still exists, though a visitor to the Synod might be excused for thinking otherwise, so wide is the spectrum of synodical concern. The implication that because it is of concern to Christians it should therefore have time in Synod is to deny the fact that Parliament has a competence, and a Christian competence, denied to the Synod itself.

The whole panoply is built upon a false premise, that the Christian Church is a democracy, and therefore should be patterned upon the mother of parliaments across the road. Here again the Church has sold itself to a generalization that democracy is a good thing, and therefore we must run democratically. The Church of God, however, is a theocracy. It is a sphere which recognizes the rule of God as supreme, a recognition made as well by the earthly Sovereign as by her subjects. It is the generalization that is wrong, not the concept of democracy. It may well be the method by which money is raised, on the principle of no taxation without representation. It may well inform the administrative structures of the Church—which it most certainly does not at the present. It may well accord with the proper place of the laity and their representation on trusts and committees of management. Yet as Mr Longley writes in his trenchant contribution, majority rule 'secularizes the process and maintains the fragmentation which is Anglicanism's major disease'.

In particular the democratic principle finds itself opposed to that of *episcope*. The architects of synodical government—and the variety under consideration is not the same as that obtaining in the early centuries of church history—chose to ignore the fact that they were trying to mix oil and water. Perhaps they overlooked the fact or wanted to change it. Instead they created a so-called democratic institution and gave it powers that were either inappropriate or ill-defined as, for example, the ordering of liturgical worship, which must belong to those areas of theology and doctrine of which the bishops, not the Synod, are the guardians. Subtly the role of bishop as centre of unity in the faith has been eroded and replaced with a hierarchy unsure on which side its bread is buttered.

Synod was seen as a co-operative enterprise between bishops, clergy and laity for legislating on the legal structures of the Church and matters of liturgy and doctrine. The House of Bishops has a rather negative hold on the last item, as Synod may propose things for the approval of the bishops, but they can return it to Synod to be accepted or rejected, but not altered. The reserve powers of the House of Bishops, though not very apparent, are therefore real if they choose to use them, and the only remedy Synod has is by voting against their proposals. On the one hand Synod accepts the authority of bishops, and on the other it has the power to overthrow it. Much depends on where the initiative lies, and this in fact largely turns on some board or committee having discussed it first. And since the boards set their own agendas they may be seen to have a determining influence upon Synod as a whole. Indeed the Standing Committee does not control the boards' demands for debate upon their reports; and the chairman of all but one board is a diocesan bishop, caught between the unresolved Scylla of episcopacy and the Charybdis of a particular form of synodical government. We hear much of the Bishop-in-Synod; we should not overlook the more fundamental concept of Bishop-in-Diocese. The Diocese is an essential part of the government of the Church and has, to a surprising degree, retained considerable independence as far as internal organization is concerned. The most significant constraint is the consequence of the centralization of the Church's funds in the Church Commissioners.

One cannot resist the conclusion that there is a proper distinction between the temporal and the spiritual, however spiritual the temporal may be thought to be. Good housekeeping of church properties, a knowledge of rising damp and efficient drains, are required of those who have particular responsibility. But they are different from the theological insight and awareness needed by the Christian minister. Perhaps its very omnicompetence is one of the Synod's failings. Certainly its claim and practice to determine matters of faith and theology are wrong in principle and disastrous in practice. The Synod tends to have ideas above its station, though a sociological study of its members might still leave one in doubt as to their function and indeed the purpose of their presence, except for that magic and widely misused word *representative*. The Christian Church would run better on more trust and less representation.

The Synod is ill-adapted to answer any but yes/no questions, and most of life is a grey area somewhere in between. Furthermore, most of life is both outside the Synod and outside the church. Should that not be the top priority, rather than pontificating on matters of national importance in so superficial a way that it commands little respect and takes far too much time? What indeed, one may well ask, are the priorities of the Synod? Or perhaps one should rather ask, who determines them? If, as one contributor states, 'The real crisis is secularism and religious indifference', then it seems that the role of Nero is closer to that of the Synod than that of Francis of Assisi. The Church of England has created a hydra-like bureaucracy, and fitted it perilously near with self-perpetuating powers. The longer it runs, the more difficult it will be to change. The time for change, therefore, is now.

We are still an episcopal Church. That is the form of government which, under God, our Church in common with other historic Churches, has joyfully accepted. As Canon John Halliburton wrote in his contribution to *Government by Synod*:

> Synodical government may be an admirable means of consultation; but it should never obscure the fact that the Anglican Communion is episcopally structured and that many are looking for a greater solidarity among the bishops (which is their right to do) and a firmer affirmation together with a clear guidance in matters which perplex ... Episcopacy is not a pass to perform certain functions, but a role within a specific community.

The comprehensiveness of the Reformation Settlement appears now to have been watered down to a free-for-all, to believe or to deny, and if the historic guardians of the faith themselves appear to have neither consensus nor common mind—it is scarcely surprising that the Church has neither as well. A seductive liberalism has removed the traditional boundary posts of theology, morality and faith.

We have given some attention to the concept of comprehensiveness which can, only too easily, become a parrot cry of the unthinking. It is, however, too serious a matter for church order to be overlooked, especially in these days of ecumenical activity. It can scarcely be claimed as the esse of the Church, nor can unthinking acceptance of it as part of Anglicanism be sustained. It is a characteristic which has enabled the Church of England to sail through troubled waters in the four centuries of its history. It is, however, quite another matter to make it an excuse for the continual holding of opposite and apparently irreconcilable views, while at the same time claiming a consensus. If the Church cannot agree for instance on matters of daily morality and basic faith, it has surely surrendered its claim to be the voice of conscience in the world. It has certainly surrendered integrity in the view of the majority of people not in the pew. How often has it been said that 'people' are going to listen in to this or that debate, or read next morning in the papers what has been said. Equally often very little is reported—which is, sometimes, as well.

Yet can the bishops any longer exercise their historic *episcope*? I believe they can—just. But the sands of time are running out. The method of their appointment was radically changed by a private agreement between Prime Minister and Archbishop and there is little conclusive evidence that this change has worked to the advantage of the Church. Slowly the Synod is assuming functions that properly belong to the bishops, and the central bureaucracy does not have that grace of Orders in the Holy Catholic Church, upon which the bishops can rely.

The Synod has now run for fifteen years. Has it succeeded in its objectives? Certainly it has enabled the laity to appear to take a larger place in the deliberations of the Church. It has fostered Ecumenism and firmly set Anglicanism in the context, not merely of the British Isles, but of the world. It has done much to support and develop social responsibility and social consciousness among Anglicans. But it has done nothing to stem the outgoing tide of church membership both in town and country or the diminishing resources of parish and diocese. Its obsession with relevance does not appear to have paid any dividends or to have challenged vocations to the ministry. It continues to spend increasingly large sums of money it does not have (many dioceses and most parishes are virtually bankrupted by quotas, contributions and other euphemisms for penal taxation) and servilely to submit to the status quo, probably because it knows it has little power to change.

Yet while it has the opportunity to change and to face its very human failings, it must do so if its credibility is to survive. Those who serve the Synod, whether as its permanent secretariat, elected officers or members, are people of integrity and good will, for the most part swept along by the ever-rising tide of ecclesiastical activism. Synod, as one of our contributors observes, 'is a sociological rather than a theological phenomenon.' It has no divine right and is as likely to err as Councils have erred (see Article XXI), and indeed churches themselves have erred 'not only in their living and manner of Ceremonies, but also in matters of Faith'. The euphoria of its birth must not lead to a mystique of Synod which rejects criticism and refuses a serious inquiry into if, and how, the General Synod of the Church of England could, and therefore should, be improved.

2

The Creation of the Synod

Eric Kemp

The General Synod came into being in 1970 some fifty years after the formation of the Church Assembly and the passing of the Enabling Act which bestowed on that body certain delegated powers of legislation. During that half century the Church Assembly, which consisted of the members of the Convocations of Canterbury and York together with a House of Laity, functioned alongside the separate, continuing meetings of the Convocations. Section 14 of its constitution provided that:

> it does not belong to the functions of the Assembly to issue any statement purporting to define the doctrine of the Church of England on any question of theology, and no such statement shall be issued by the Assembly.

Section 15 provided that:

> Nothing in this Constitution shall be deemed to diminish or derogate from any of the powers belonging to the Convocations of the Provinces of Canterbury and York or of any House thereof.

The Convocations of Canterbury and York were and are the ancient provincial synods of the two provinces in which the Church of England has, at least in principle, been organized since the arrival of St Augustine at the end of the sixth century. As the Christian gospel was preached throughout the Mediterranean world and local churches were established these gradually grouped themselves into provinces on the lines of the secular organization of the Roman Empire. This ecclesiastical organization was recognized by the Council of Nicaea in AD 325 which ordered councils or synods of each province to meet twice a year.

Such synods were composed essentially of the bishops of the province and acted both as courts of law, hearing and determining

10

disputes in the province, and as legislative bodies making canons or regulations for the province which, however, were always seen as subject to the tradition and legislation of the whole Church. The bishops generally brought with them others of the clergy as their advisers and in some countries at certain periods the business of the synods was often done in mixed ecclesiastical and lay assemblies under the oversight of the secular ruler.

In England separate meetings of the two provinces are not clearly distinguishable until some time after the Norman Conquest, but after the Fourth Lateran Council in 1215 had renewed the Nicene rule of two provincial synods a year, evidence of such meetings, though not with that frequency, appears for both provinces. By then the attendance of others than bishops was beginning to be formalized. Cathedral chapters had acquired the right to be summoned; archdeacons, abbots and priors of the larger religious houses were often present, and sometimes theologians from the universities.

In the course of the thirteenth century these synods were affected by a new development, namely the taxation of the clergy to provide royal and papal revenue. The pope was regarded as having the right to require taxes, though various ways of resisting or evading were developed. The kings had to ask for and receive consent to taxation. This led to the two archbishops summoning special assemblies for this purpose and at such assemblies it was necessary to have representatives of all the tax-paying bodies, coming with power to bind those whom they represented. So in addition to the bishops, there were summoned deans and priors of the cathedrals with proctors from their chapters, abbots and priors of many monasteries, the archdeacons and two elected representatives (proctors) of the clergy of each diocese. The frequent summoning of these taxing assemblies had an influence on the attendance of other clergy in addition to the bishops at provincial synods. By the end of the fourteenth century the two had become fused and the lower clergy (including the elected proctors) had acquired the right both to be summoned and to give or withhold consent in relation to a wider range of business than just taxation. These assemblies were still the provincial synods but the name which became more often used for them was Convocation of the Clergy. Each Convocation was divided into two houses, an Upper House consisting of the bishops and certain abbots and priors, and a

11

Lower House consisting of the rest of those summoned.

Because of the taxing functions of the Convocations, they were usually summoned by the archbishops at the direction of the king contained in a royal writ, the writ usually being recited in the archbishop's own citation of the bishops and through them of the lower clergy. In 1532 the Convocations made what is known as the Submission of the Clergy, by which they undertook not to make any new canons without the royal assent and asked for a commission to review existing canons, those approved by the commission to be put in force with the royal assent. They also acknowledged that they should only meet by authority of the king's writ. Two years later the Convocations agreed that the Roman pontiff had no greater jurisdiction in the realm of England given him by God in Holy Scripture, than any other foreign bishop. After 1539 there were no longer any abbots or priors or other religious to sit in the Convocations.

The Convocations continued to be summoned and to be involved in most of the changes which took place between 1540 and 1640, and after the Commonwealth they were summoned again in 1661 and the present Book of Common Prayer was synodically subscribed on 20 December 1661. Three years later Archbishop Sheldon, by oral agreement with Lord Chancellor Clarendon, surrendered the right of the clergy to tax themselves in Convocation. Now the Convocations were of no particular use to the government. They continued to be summoned along with each new parliament but were quickly prorogued and did no business. After a brief revival in 1689 they resumed a formal existence until the reign of Queen Anne when they were again allowed to debate and to transact business. Disputes between the Upper and Lower Houses about their respective rights caused some difficulties but gradually it seemed as if some positive reform of the discipline of the Church was in prospect when doctrinal disputes began. At first these united bishops and clergy in the condemnation of the Arian doctrine of William Whiston, but this led on to an attack by the Lower House on the teaching of Benjamin Hoadley, Bishop of Bangor. By now the Queen had died and the Hanoverian dynasty had arrived. Hoadley was a Whig supporter, many of his opponents were Tories and suspected of Jacobitism, and in 1717 the government suspended the proceedings of Convocation. By now the Convocation of York had almost faded away and one writer described it as the hands of a clock whose works are at Canterbury. Except for a brief moment in 1741 the Convocations were not allowed to meet for business again for over a hundred years.

The events of the sixteenth and seventeenth centuries were based on two theories, as far as their effect on Church government was concerned. One was that a Christian ruler has the right to oversee and control the activities of the Church in his dominions. The other was that the voice of the laity of the Church finds its expression in Parliament, and more particularly in the House of Commons. Thus the major Reformation changes were embodied in Acts of Parliament, though many of the more important, as we have seen, were also agreed to by the clergy in Convocation. As a result of the Submission of the Clergy the Convocations could only meet in consequence of the issue of a royal writ and could only make canons by royal licence, but it was accepted that the king could not himself directly summon the Convocations and by-pass the archbishops in so doing. Like the election of bishops the ancient legislative machinery of the Church remained intact but enclosed within the constraints of royal power without whose consent it could not operate.

Those who were responsible for what was done in this period of change did not think of themselves as innovating in religion but rather as restoring a purer form of Christianity as it had existed in the early Church before it was overlaid by medieval superstition and papal usurpation. Thus the threefold order of ministry of bishops, priests and deacons was carefully continued and the Supremacy Act of 1559 contains the following passage which illustrates the limits within which Parliament felt itself to be working. The clause provides that such person or persons to whom the Queen gives authority to have or execute any jurisdiction, power or authority spiritual

> shall not in any wise have authority or power to order, determine, or adjudge any matter or cause to be heresy, but only such as heretofore have been determined, ordered, or adjudged to be heresy, by the authority of the canonical Scriptures, or by the first four general Councils, or any of them, or by any other general Council wherein the same was declared heresy by the express and plain words of the said canonical Scriptures, or such as hereafter shall be ordered, judged, or determined to be heresy

13

by the High Court of Parliament of this realm, with the assent of the clergy in their Convocations.

The suitability of Parliament to represent the laity of the Church began to be called in question early in the nineteenth century. This was partly the result of the marked increase in ecclesiastical legislation by Parliament without consultation with the Convocations. Between 1760 and 1820 the annual average of ecclesiastical statutes was ten. Between 1820 and 1870 it was twenty-five. The questioning was also the result, however, of the repeal of the Test and Corporation Acts in 1828 and Roman Catholic Emancipation in 1829, the effect of which was that the House of Commons ceased to be a body of lay members of the Established Church. A movement began for a revival of the Convocations and it was led by a representative body of churchpeople, clerical and lay. It was not a purely High Church movement.

In the middle of the century, pressure had built up sufficiently to cause the government to allow the Convocations to meet for debate and resolution and to issue letters of business for some revision of the canons. There were, however, those who maintained that an assembly which did not include the laity could not function satisfactorily as a central assembly of the Church. In 1884 this feeling brought about the setting up of House of Laymen which should meet at the same time as the Convocations and should be consulted, more particularly about matters needing parliamentary legislation and in 1898 provision was made for joint meetings in London of the two provincial Houses of Laymen. In the same year a Joint Committee of the two Convocations was set up to consider the position of the laity in church government, historically and theologically. The Committee's conclusion about the place of the laity in the early church was and remains important:

> We believe that there is a primitive distinction between clergy and laity, and that it will continue to the end of the age in which we live. This distinction is involved in the choice and commission of the Apostles: and its continuance is implied in our Lord's words to them connecting their work with His second coming ... But by distinction we do not understand separation as of bodies with opposing interests. We have no reason to regard the distinction as anything more than a provision for the purpose of developing the fulness of corporate life in the Church which is

14

Christ's body, and for maintaining in it the fulness of truth. Nay, we perceive very clearly, both from the historical and the theological portions of the New Testament, that the ultimate authority and the right of collective action lie with the whole body, the Church. We find, in fact, in this first period traces of the co-operation of clergy and laity in all the three spheres with which our Report is concerned, in legislative functions, in the election of Church officers, and in judicial discipline, and we cannot but conclude that this co-operation belongs to the true ideal of the Church.

The Report recommended the formation of a National Council fully representing the clergy and laity of the Church of England and in 1903 the Representative Church Council, in effect the two Convocations and the two Houses of Laymen meeting together, was set up. The problem of parliamentary legislation on church matters remained and was becoming more acute as parliamentary time became less and less. In 1913 therefore, on the recommendation of the Council, a commission was set up to examine this problem; it recommended in 1916 that a body similar to the Representative Church Council be established and be given power to legislate for the Church, such legislation being subject only to the veto of Parliament and of the Crown.

Immediately after the end of the First World War these recommendations were carried into effect, largely because they were pressed by the Life and Liberty Movement led by William Temple and others. The Church Assembly, consisting of the two Convocations and a House of Laity, was set up by act of the Convocations and was endowed by the Enabling Act of 1919, with the right to pass measures concerning ecclesiastical matters which were then presented to both Houses of Parliament to be accepted or rejected, without power of revision, on a simple motion. If passed they received the royal assent and became part of the statute law of England.

As we saw at the beginning of this chapter the constitution of the Church Assembly expressly safeguarded the position of the Convocations, the result being that when any question of the doctrine of the church arose or of entering into a relationship of communion with another Church it was reserved to the Convocations, subject to the fact that if a change in the statute law was involved such

15

change had also to go through the Church Assembly and Parliament.

Along with the creation of the Church Assembly a structure of Diocesan Conferences, Ruridecanal Conferences and Parochial Church Councils was also set up, in all of which the laity sat alongside the clergy.

The passing of the Enabling Act certainly eased the problem of getting ecclesiastical legislation through Parliament and many long overdue reforms in church organization were made. The rejection of the Revised Prayer Book by the House of Commons in 1927 and again in 1928 and the rejection of the proposal for a diocese of Shrewsbury by the House of Lords shortly afterwards brought home to churchpeople that what had happened was a simplification of procedure and not that grant of freedom for which the Life and Liberty Movement had worked. The Archbishops set up a Commission on the Relations of Church and State which reported in 1935 and recommended that the freedom of legislation without recourse to Parliament which is possessed by the Established Church of Scotland should be sought for the Church of England also. The Second World War, however, intervened before consideration of this proposal had gone very far.

After the end of the war the Convocations embarked on what proved to be a long-drawn out and tedious process of revision of the Canon Law. It was realized at an early stage that many, if not most of the matters being discussed directly affected the laity and so, although the Church Assembly had no constitutional place in the making of canons, a procedure was devised by which each canon at each stage of its progress was laid before the House of Laity of the Assembly. This not only created a bottleneck which greatly slowed down the procedure but also led to friction and misunderstanding as there was no way by which canons could be discussed by the Convocations and the laity together.

In 1953 a commission was appointed to consider how the laity could best be joined with the clergy in the synodical government of the Church. It reported in 1958 with the proposal that Houses of Laity be attached to the two Convocations with rights similar to those possessed by the existing Lower Houses. This proposal met opposition both from those who objected to it on principle and those who believed it to be cumbrous and wanted something simpler. Four years of debate, committees and reports led in 1963 to a vote in the Church Assembly which seemed to indicate sufficient agreement on a way forward for another commission to be set up, the Synodical Government Commission under the chairmanship of Lord Hodson. Their Report was published in 1966, discussed not only in the Church Assembly but also in the Diocesan Conferences and led to the framing and passing of the Synodical Government Measure which brought the General Synod into being in 1970.

The Measure represents a compromise agreement between different points of view in the Church. One extreme view advocated the abolition of the Convocations entirely. An opposing view wished the Convocations to have a complete veto on the proceedings of the General Synod in certain areas, notably worship and doctrine. A further complication was the desire to prevent the distinctive ethos of the Northern Province from being completely swallowed up by the much larger Province of Canterbury.

Those who wished the Convocations to be retained emphasized the special responsibilities of teaching and guardianship of the faith that are shared by the bishops and the clergy. They contrasted the procedure of the Convocations which allowed such matters to be discussed thoroughly and at length with the pressure of time which so often bore heavily on major debates in the Church Assembly. Along with that was the fact that the York Lower House had more than once showed itself somewhat conservative as against a more radical line taken by a majority in the Canterbury Convocation. It was feared that a Synod which did not contain the checks and balances of the four Houses of Convocation might make major changes in doctrine and worship to the great distress of substantial minorities. Experience since 1970 has shown that that fear was not unjustified.

The Synodical Government Measure retains the Convocations. They are elected as such, they continue to meet separately from time to time and their Presidents and Prolocutors have the right to require separate discussion in the Convocations of certain matters. Their power of making canons has, however, been transferred to the General Synod. The Convocations can delay but they cannot finally prevent legislation from passing the General Synod. Questions of worship and doctrine are intended to be safeguarded by procedures which require reference to the dioceses and special majorities in each House of the Synod at a certain stage, as well as

17

by the requirement that the final vote must be on a proposal from the House of Bishops.

The Synodical Government Measure also revised the structure of diocesan and deanery assemblies. Many of the diocesan conferences were very large bodies, some having more than a thousand members, and in consequence were not suitable as debating assemblies. There was also criticism of the Church Assembly, which had about 750 members, from that point of view. The Synodical Government Commission was charged to look at this problem and spent some time in consulting expert witnesses in procedures of government. In the end it tried to fix the General Synod membership at about 500 and the diocesan synods at about 200. At once the question arose of how far the reduced numbers could make the synods reasonably representative of church opinion, and that especially with regard to the presentation of legislation to Parliament. For this reason the deanery synods were given a more important function than the former ruridecanal conferences had had. Their numbers were to be round about a hundred and in any case not less than fifty. The laity in the deanery synods were to be and are the electors of lay representatives not only to the diocesan synod but also to the General Synod. All beneficed and licensed clergy of a deanery elect clerical representatives to the diocesan synod, and all beneficed and licensed clergy of the diocese elect the proctors who represent them in the Convocations and General Synod.

Article 8 of the Constitution of the General Synod provides that certain matters must be referred to the dioceses and be approved by a majority of the dioceses at meetings of their diocesan synods before being given final approval by the General Synod. It has become usual, and is sometimes explicitly required by the General Synod, that on the occasion of such references deanery synods are consulted before the diocesan synod takes it decision. Such matters are defined in the Constitution as:

A Measure or Canon providing for permanent changes in the Services of Baptism or Holy Communion or in the Ordinal, or a scheme for a constitutional union or a permanent and substantial change of relationship between the Church of England and another Christian body, being a body a substantial number of whose members reside in Great Britain.

The same Article provides also that the General Synod may require at the stage of final approval of such a scheme special majorities in each House, or in the whole Synod, or in both. Permanent changes in Baptism, Holy Communion and the Ordinal require a majority in each House of the Synod of not less than two-thirds of those present and voting.

Article 7 of the Constitution states that a provision touching doctrinal formulae or the services or ceremonies of the Church of England or the administration of the Sacraments or sacred rites thereof shall, before final approval, be referred to the House of Bishops and be submitted for final approval only in terms proposed by that House. The Article further provides that if either of the Convocations or the House of Laity so requires such matters shall be referred to them in the terms proposed by the House of Bishops and shall not be submitted for final approval until it has been approved by each House of Convocation, sitting separately, and by the House of Laity. If such a proposal fails to secure approval in this way it cannot be introduced again until a new General Synod comes into being. In the case of rejection by one House of Convocation only there can be a second reference and in the case of a second objection by one House only the proposal goes to the Houses of Bishops and Clergy of the General Synod for approval by a two-thirds majority of each House present and voting in lieu of approval by the four Houses of Convocation.

Alongside these two Articles must be set certain requirements of the Worship and Doctrine Measure (1974) dealing with the approval of services alternative to those in the Book of Common Prayer and some other matters concerning the services of the Church. Every canon or regulation made under this Measure must be passed by a two-thirds majority of those present and voting in each House of the Synod.

Taken together these various provisions constitute an attempt to protect the Church against such changes in its doctrine and order as would be felt by a substantial minority to undermine its position as a true part of Christ's Holy Catholic Church. During the fifteen years of the Synod's existence there have been and continue to be attempts to whittle them away. Three examples may be given. In 1972, when the proposals for Anglican-Methodist Unity were presented for final approval it was agreed that they should require both a two-thirds majority in each House and a majority of 75% in

19

the Synod overall. In 1981 when the procedure for voting on the Proposals for a Covenant was discussed, the Synod accepted a two-thirds majority in each House but refused to require an overall percentage of seventy-five, and indeed any overall percentage at all. More recently there has been the proposal that women ordained priests in other parts of the Anglican communion should be allowed to function as priests when visiting this country. Opponents of the proposal argued that to accept this would be to accept in principle the rightness of the ordination of women to the priesthood, and for that reason it was declared to come under the Article 8 procedure. Supporters of the proposal then, at the Revision Stage, introduced an amendment to limit its operation to seven years and argued that because it was not a permanent change the provisions of Article 8 did not apply. They failed in their contention but the incident illustrates the determination of a section of the Synod to do away with the checks and safeguards of the Constitution.

A third example may be found in the argument recently put forward that an Enabling Measure does not fall under the Article 8 provisions even though the canons which it enables to be made do. Such an argument would allow the Synod to pass without the Article 8 procedure a Measure enabling it to make a canon which did away with the requirement of episcopal ordination. It would seem ludicrous that in such a case the principle could be settled without the Article 8 procedure whereas the practical application required it. Constant vigilance is needed to protect the integrity of the faith and order of the Church.

Reference to the Worship and Doctrine Measure of 1974 takes us back to the question of the Church and Parliament. Mention has already been made of the Commission on the Relations of Church and State which reported in 1935. It was a weighty Commission and produced a substantial document which is still worthy of attention. It proposed that the freedom of legislation, of election of officers and judicial discipline enjoyed by the Church of Scotland should be seriously considered for the Church of England. By contrast the next commission on Church and State appointed in 1949 was faint-hearted indeed. Its members were not even able to agree that a status similar to that of the Church of Scotland should be the ultimate goal of the Church's long-term policy. From this Commission, however, resulted the first statutory authorization for the provision of services alternative to those in the Book of Common Prayer without recourse to Parliament, though this authorization was limited to a period of sixteen years.

It was in part the realization that the expiry of that period was drawing near which led to the next Church and State Commission which reported in 1970. Its first recommendation was that 'All matters affecting the worship and doctrine of the Church should become subject to the final authority of the General Synod, with certain safeguards provided.' The safeguards proposed chiefly concerned worship and these as eventually translated into legislation in the Worship and Doctrine Measure entrenched the services in the Book of Common Prayer to be permanently available but gave the General Synod power to change the rubrics and to provide alternative services without limit of time, subject to the requirement of a two-thirds majority in each House of the Synod for each canon or regulation made under the Measure, as has already been stated.

As regards doctrine, the Commission proposed that a measure should empower the General Synod to prescribe by canon the obligations of the clergy and certain lay officers to subscribe to the doctrine of the Church, and the forms of that subscription; and also to interpret by canon the formularies of the Church. This too was translated into legislation in the Worship and Doctrine Measure with again the requirement of a two-thirds majority for changes in the form of subscription or Declaration of Assent.

There is also in the Measure a further safeguard in the requirement that every canon or regulation and every form of service or amendment thereof made under the Measure 'shall be such as in the opinion of the General Synod is neither contrary to, nor indicative of any departure from, the doctrine of the Church of England in any essential matter.' In a later clause it is stated that references in the Measure to the doctrine of the Church of England are to be construed in accordance with Canon A 5 which states that:

> The doctrine of the Church of England is grounded in the holy Scriptures, and in such teachings of the ancient Fathers and Councils of the Church as are agreeable to the said Scriptures. In particular such doctrine is to be found in the Thirty-nine Articles of Religion, the Book of Common Prayer, and the Ordinal.

The Measure also states in relation to the phrase about 'the opinion of the General Synod' quoted in the previous paragraph that:

> The final approval by the General Synod of any such Canon or regulation or form of service or amendment thereof shall conclusively determine that the Synod is of such opinion as aforesaid with respect to the matter so approved.

This has been read by some as if it meant that the expressed opinion of the Synod is conclusive of whether any change is or is not contrary to or indicative of a departure from the doctrine of the Church of England. It is, however, at least doubtful whether such a reading of the clause is correct, and it would seem possible that the opinion of the General Synod on any matter could be challenged in the courts or in Parliament. Practically speaking, nevertheless, the General Synod has acquired an almost complete control over the doctrine of the Church and this makes even more disturbing the repeated attempts to whittle away safeguards which have already been noted.

During the long years of discussion which led up to the creation of the General Synod and the bestowing on it of its present powers certain concerns are repeatedly apparent. The most prominent was the need for revision of forms of worship without continual recourse to Parliament, and along with that the possibility of being able to settle a host of practical matters relating to churches and worship without cumbrous legislation. Another matter of concern was the appointment to office in the Church and the terms on which office is to be held. Also in mind were some of the questions that might arise in the course of progress towards Christian unity. There does not appear to have been any expectation that the General Synod might attempt to make major changes in the doctrine and order of the Church and the safeguards provided were considered adequate to prevent it from doing so. Their inadequacy and the attempts made to circumvent them are therefore a cause of widespread anxiety in the Church.

The late Dr Iremonger, who had been closely associated with William Temple in the Life and Liberty Movement and was subsequently Director of Religious Broadcasting and then Dean of Lichfield, observed of the Church Assembly that it had never really come to a clear decision as to what was its role in the Church.

As we have seen the primary purpose in setting up the Assembly was that it should be endowed by the Enabling Act with legislative powers. Its procedure for that reason was closely modelled on that of Parliament. There was, however, a body of opinion which saw the Assembly as 'the voice of the Church' on great national and moral issues. There was in consequence competition for the time of the Assembly and some members stood for election by reason of their interest in the legislation whereas others were more concerned with the wider debates.

This duality of role has been inherited by the General Synod but the congestion of business that follows from it has been made worse by the creation of a substantial structure of boards and councils which work away at various fields of interest and produce reports to be debated by the Synod. There has been a growing tendency for these reports to be sent down to the dioceses and deaneries for discussion and with a date set by which the dioceses must produce a reply. In recent years this feature along with an increase in the legislation which has to be referred under Article 8 has, at the time of writing, reached a point at which many of the deanery synods are rebelling and saying that they simply have not time to deal adequately with this plethora of General Synod references and that they are being prevented by it from devoting that thought and care for the work and mission of the Church in the deanery which is the primary duty laid upon them by the Synodical Government Measure.

Attempts by the House of Bishops to reduce the amount of business brought to the Synod and the time taken by it have failed, individual protests by bishops and others go unheeded, but unless the boards and councils restrict their activities and individual members of the Synod restrain themselves in putting down motions there is danger of serious damage to the mission of the Church in the dioceses.

A possible solution would be to limit the business of the Synod to legislation and matters directly connected with it, thus reducing the amount of time taken and perhaps making it possible to have only two instead of three groups of sessions a year. That would have the additional advantage of slowing down legislation. It might then be practicable to revive something like the Church Congress which could meet every two or three years for a week or ten days, with a wider membership than the Synod, and could debate at length some of the more important issues concerning the life of Church and nation and perhaps in some cases prepare the way for legislation in the Synod.

Above all at the present time is the need for the General Synod to face squarely and accept its responsibility to the historic faith and order of the Church.

3

A Question of Confidence

Hugh Craig

When George Goyder moved his motion in the Church Assembly in 1953 which began the long haul to synodical government, he quoted these opening words from the 1902 Canterbury Convocation Report on the position of the laity:

> The Church of the apostolic age was neither democratic nor despotic. Not democratic: for the pleasure of the multitude was not the ultimate sanction of the office of its leaders. Not despotic: for its officers were not lords over subjects, but divinely commissioned leaders of a divine society of brethren. What it was in general idea may be best expressed by the word 'collective' or 'corporate'. The life and action of the Church were the life and action of the whole body. The officers acted with, not instead of, the community; and the community acted with, not in mere obedience under, its officers. Still less could it supersede or act apart from them. The principle follows directly from the truth that the Holy Spirit was given to the body as a whole. In nothing less than the whole body does the fulness of the Spirit reside— for illumination or for power.

Certainly the ideal which motivated the introduction of synodical government was to allow 'the whole body'—and especially the whole of the body of the laity—to participate in the government of the Church. Doubtless some less worthy thoughts of administrative convenience—after the comic unwieldiness of the Canon Law revision process—intruded. How far has this been achieved? How far is there confidence in the new system among the laity?

Before an answer can be attempted, we have first to face the apparently simple, but actually intractable question—who are the laity? Simplistic answers like '99% of the Church', or 'the Church minus the clergy' will not do. Ecclesiastical answers like 'the baptized', 'the confirmed', or 'regular communicants' are not good enough. Some of those baptized openly reject the Christian faith, and when is a communicant a 'regular' one? Prayer Book answers like 'the blessed company of all faithful believers' have the merit of being theologically exact: but do not help too much in practical identification. Indeed the problem is the one the Articles grapple with when they speak of the 'visible' Church of Christ which is at best an approximation to the 'invisible' Church, or better that real Church whose bounds are known only to God.

The electoral base

The synodical system sought to solve the problem by equating the electorate with revised electoral rolls in each parish, updated triennially. Much was made of the change that this would make from the older electoral rolls, which were supposed to contain much 'dead wood'. In my own limited experience the difference was there, but it was not dramatic: though doubtless this varied somewhat from parish to parish. These electoral rolls were to form the electorate at Annual Church Meetings, which elected representatives to deanery synods. These representatives would in turn elect the House of Laity of the General Synod. The theory seemed sound enough.

In practice the system has two defects. The first relates to the electoral roll. It is not co-extensive with the 'visible' or the 'invisible' Church. Furthermore—and much more important—the electoral roll is by no means co-extensive with those who attend Annual Church Meetings. To be sure, we can complain that they ought to attend: but the fallen world is full of imperfections. Many good Christian folk—more than we often recognize—find their vocation in their daily employment and are impatient of the trivia of many an Annual Meeting, and even sometimes of the irrelevance of local church activities to real life or real faith. They are, of course, to be blamed: but not more than those who use the local church as an escape from that real world where truth and justice have to be contended for, 'not without dust and heat', or those who try and turn their local church into a private sect which unchurches godly folk with whom they happen to disagree!

The second defect relates to the nature of deanery synods. These derived their importance in the Hodson Commission scheme as the electorate of the General Synod House of Laity. Every parish was represented on them: and the franchise was to be wide enough to impress Parliament. But alas, the deanery synods, having elected the House of Laity, and their representatives of the diocesan synod and its subordinate bodies, and perhaps allocated quotas, have no other powers, unless parishes cede them by consent. They are mere talking-shops, and often in some difficulty to discover what to talk about. Some are well-run, and the weakness scarcely shows. Others are less well-run, and it has become increasingly difficult to find people to sit on them. While I in no way wish to condone the failure of many laity to understand and take advantage of the opportunity that synodical government gives to them, one has in fairness to confess that on occasion lay members of the deanery synod have to be asked to stand by their local vicar. This is scarcely in the spirit of true lay representation. As a result of all this, those who do stand are not necessarily those who in the elections to the General Synod can best reflect the views of the real parish laity.

There is much work to be done to arouse the laity to take advantage of the opportunities that synodical government has given to them. It might help if real tasks were to be given to the House of Laity of the deanery synods: and if they, at least once a year, met on their own. For instance we could charge the House of Laity of each deanery synod to consider the effectiveness of the Church in their deanery in evangelism, in teaching the faith, in bringing its influence to bear on local life, and in ministering to the needy, and to report back to their PCCs.

Lay representation in the General Synod

Granted then that the system has weaknesses, are those who reach the General Synod representative of the laity at parish level? Some analysis of those elected has been carried out, notably that analysis reported in *Crucible* by Professor Kathleen Jones and George Moyser[1]. To this professional analysis I have added, for comparison, a rough analysis carried out by George Goyder, and reported by him to the Church Assembly in 1953[2], and an even more rough analysis carried out by myself on the information given in the Church of England Year Book. The data are summarized on the following page.

The only significant trends—which anyone in the Synod with a long memory will confirm without needing surveys—are that the

Composition of the House of Laity of Assembly/General Synod

	Rough 1953 Analysis	1970 Survey	1975 Survey	1980 Survey	Rough 1981 Analysis
Age Distribution					
Sample of House	—	94%	94.7%	69%	—
Under 40	—	23%	9.4%	9.6%	12.1%
40–59	—	48%	65%	58%	56.5%
Over 60	—	29%	25.6%	32.4%	31.3%*
Over 65	25.8%	—	—	—	15.2%
New Members	—	54%	50.6%	—	—
Women (% of Whole House)					
Clergy Wives	6.6%	—	6.0%	—	6.8%
Nuns & Deaconesses	—	—	3.0%	—	4.6%
Other F/T Church Workers	—	—	3.9%	—	2.5%
Other Women	—	—	18.4%	—	21.5%
Total Women	22.2%	21.7%	31.3%	37%	35.4%
Men (% of Whole House)					
Medical	1%				5.9%
Account/Survey	4.5%				3.4%
Civil S/Local G	3.3%				3.4%
Law	5.4%				5.1%
Education	5.7%				13.8%
Rtd Services	3.6%				3.0%
MPs	1.2%				0.8%
Trade Union	0.6%				N.A
Farming	2.7%				3.0%
Industry ⎫ Business ⎬ Banking ⎭	5.7%				18.6%
Journalism	0.3%				1.7%
Professional Church Workers	5.7%				1.3%

* includes those over 65

very poor representation from the business world of the old
Church Assembly has been somewhat redressed; that the
universities and schools are increasingly over-represented (including both sexes and the retired they are now 18.5% of the House)
and that the increase in womens' representation has been dispro-
portionately in deaconesses, nuns, other full-time church workers
and clergy wives, rather than in representatives of ordinary women
in the parishes. Something like one-sixth of the members of the
House of Laity are in fact, in one way or another, in the Church's
employ.

Quite apart from any question of trends, the composition of the
House, as indicated in the above table, invites other comments.
One cannot really quarrel with Professor Jones' conclusion that the
Synod is 'far more like an ecclesiastical British Academy than a
representative body'—if by representative body she means a cross-
section of the laity in the pews or on the electoral rolls. Unfortunately no similar analysis, so far as I am aware, has been carried out
on the laity of the deanery synods. One suspects that the House of
Laity may be a reasonable cross-section of the more articulate laity
on the deanery synods: but that the laity on those synods do not
fully reflect, as argued above, some of the strands of opinion of the
believing laity at large. It is by no means impossible that those
strands are as well represented in Parliament as they are in the
General Synod.

The age distribution of the Synod, and over-representation of
those in Church employ, clergy wives, and the retired is only to be
expected when one considers the time demands made on those
elected. It is difficult for those in ordinary employment to find the
time needed, even if they sacrifice much of their holidays. What
tends to happen is that such people, when elected, are unable to
contribute as much as the more leisured to work on boards,
councils and committees. Their influence is thereby lessened.

The influence of the laity on the General Synod is also lessened
by the high turnover in the membership of the House of Laity. As
the above table shows, about half of the House is new each election.
As it takes time to get used to the Synod's procedures and to find
the best way to make one's contribution, it follows that a substantial number of the House never make an effective contribution.
The cause of the high turnover is a matter of speculation. The high
time demands of the Synod encourage a disproportionate number

of retired people to stand. The same time demands often discour-
age younger members as family commitments grow. The turnover
is also influenced by disenchantment with the Synod, and by the
fact that a minority of the House were unsuitable candidates for
such work from the outset.

Elections of the General Synod House of Laity

Let us next consider how the electoral system to the House of Laity
works. Candidates are chosen, in practice, on the basis of election
addresses which are circulated, on the basis of already being known
to the electorate, and (in some dioceses) on the impressions formed
at local 'hustings' organized by the diocese. I have stood successfully at eight elections, and have represented six dioceses.
I can therefore fairly claim to have some knowledge of how the
system works, at least from the candidate's point of view. Study of
elections and their results leads increasingly to a single conclusion:
lay electors in general vote for the candidates who appear to be the
most competent—those who deal best with questions at the hustings, or those who write the most competent election addresses. A
few, but only a few, are elected mainly because they are well
known: but then this distinction is blurred, since the well-known
and the competent may tend to be the same people. The lay
electors are not strongly affected by issues, which some try so
assiduously to foster at election-time. Even a highly emotive issue
like the Anglican-Methodist proposals—as far as could be judged
by the transfer of votes in the election process in the diocese I was
then in—seemed to dominate in the choice of only 10–20% of the
electors: though of course anyone strongly espousing widely-
disliked views should not be confident of election! Now, if this be
true, as I believe it is, there can be no guarantee on any subject that
the views expressed by those lay men and women elected correspond other than in general terms to those of the electorate. There is
no equivalent to the Parliamentary election manifesto, with the
consequential election primarily of the party rather than of the
man. Church parties influence clerical elections: they do not play a
large part in lay ones. It is true that the Open Synod Group has
fought elections with a national manifesto: but their success was
limited, and the electorate unimpressed by the method. Church

electors seem to vote for the person, not for the details of his policy.

The Laity and the General Synod Agenda

But there is another reason why issues do not play too large a part in lay elections. Many of the issues so dear in General Synod circles—because they reflect the interests of bishops, the clergy, the boards and councils, or even Church House,—do not have priority in the thinking of ordinary laity. They see problems at parochial and local level: and I do not write that as a criticism. It is, after all, at the local and parish level that much of the real work of the Church is done. They are concerned with the teaching and upbringing of the young. They are concerned with the standards that are taught, and are accepted in the community. They are concerned with the struggle between good and evil in local life and in their place of work, or with the problems of unemployment. They are concerned with personal troubles and those of their community. They are concerned with whether the local parish priests or the Methodist ministers, are godly men, good teachers, or helpful pastors: not with their ecclesiastical pedigree or issues of the validity of their orders. They are concerned with learning to apply the real faith they have received to the real life they have to live: not with the theological niceties of academic speculation.

It is true that deanery synods from time to time debate issues sent down to them by the General Synod. That is a costly business. Reference of a matter down to deanery level will involve the use of at least 50,000 and more likely 100,000 man-hours of time. It provokes the question whether the time could not be more usefully spent in the service of the Kingdom. The matters frequently come to the deanery synods in simplified form: and the issues are explained or expounded with varying degrees of adequacy. But the deanery synod knows that it is not its vote which matters—only that at diocesan level. Laity are far too intelligent to be fooled by the appearance of power without the substance. To try and use them as a rubber stamp is insulting and theologically offensive. Real concern with issues at General Synod level will only come if major reform (of method not constitution) makes that Synod agenda responsive to the issues laity care for. Only that way will

31

'the life and action' of the Synod become what it is not at present 'the life and action of the whole body'.

But is this criticism fair? Surely, the enthusiast for the present system will argue, the laity have all the opportunity they need. Matters can be filtered up from PCC to deanery synod, to diocese and General Synod. The fact that so few follow this route is evidence that the laity are by and large content. I think not. To them the world of the General Synod is another, and they think (no doubt wrongly) a not very important world. And the dice are stacked against them. At deanery synod they come as disparate little groups from each parish. The clergy still meet in Chapter, and can act cohesively on occasion. The laity rarely meet together in a manner where a common mind might form. And the process of feeding a motion up is so time-consuming, so indirect, with control lost at some stage unless the parish or deanery has a General Synod member among them, that the effort is usually deemed not to be worth while.

The role of the laity in the General Synod

Granted then that the representation of the laity in the General Synod has some room for improvement, let us look at the role of the laity in the Synod itself. For here the laity are free to take part in discussions with the clergy and bishops on all issues. It was here that the principal changes were made: here that the 'position of the laity' was to be put right, so that the 'life and action' might be that of the 'whole body'.

There is a perverseness about the affairs of fallen man which means that things are not always what they seem. Side by side with the constitutional changes came administrative ones which tended to produce a counter-effect. In the old Church Assembly the clergy pretended that the laity had no say in doctrine: and doctrine was debated only in Convocation. But Convocation had no power to enact canons which were contrary to statute law. Therefore if they wished—as not infrequently they did—to change statute law, the House of Laity were in the discussion as of right. The clergy made the best of the situation by inviting the House of Laity to debate the issues in parallel (more or less—though there was a time delay) with Convocation. Frequent meetings of the House of Laity on its own took place in connection with Canon Law Revision and the early stages of producing Alternative Services. This had the effect of the laity debating with themselves, and on a number of occasions a 'lay-mind' developed—such as the desire for unitive services that all major schools of thought could use.

With the advent of synodical government the House has met on its own only rarely,—and this indeed has been the wish of the majority of its members. They wished understandably to get away from the unwieldiness of the old procedure, and to make the new one work as efficiently as possible. But with the clergy and laity no longer sitting apart—and indeed many of the clergy appearing in lay attire—and the addition to the House of Bishops of some suffragans, the laity have become a mere 45% of the whole body without a distinctive voice. If one (perhaps unkindly) regards those in the Church's employ, and clergy wives, as not quite grass-roots laity, then the grass-roots representation sinks to nearer 37%—representing, after all, numerically 99% of the Church. Under these circumstances a distinctive lay voice rarely has the opportunity to emerge. Now often this does not matter—on many issues the opinion of the laity and of the clergy will be broadly similar. But just sometimes it does matter: and it is on such issues that the emergence and understanding of the different perceptions of the clergy and laity is important in deciding what action the Church, in the name of 'the whole body' ought to take. To be sure, the lay position is in part protected by procedures which allow, and sometimes demand, a vote by Houses—though even this is under increasing attack. But the point is not that the laity are out-voted. It is that their views are not adequately represented in debate. Is this fair? I take down at random a recent *Report of Proceedings* and check. 14% of the speeches were made by the bishops (9.5% of the Synod), 54% by the clergy (45% of the Synod), and 32% by the laity. Was this typical? Not quite. But the average of three sessions taken at random makes the lay contribution only 38% of the speeches: and if one excludes clergy wives and those in the employ of the Church, it drops to barely above 30%. The proportion of practising Anglican laymen who speak in the House of Commons may not be as different from the proportion who speak in the General Synod as some imagine!

Changes in procedure

It is not however only in the field of participation in debate that the role of the laity has been effectively weakened. New procedures—in the interests of streamlining, because of the pressure on the agenda, a subject to which I will return later, were introduced. The Revision stage of Measures was largely taken off the floor of the House, and committed to Revision Committees. These, like all appointed committees were chosen by a sub-committee of the Standing Committee: and although attempts are made to make them representative, success cannot be ensured. Depending on the complexity of the measure and the number of amendments proposed, these committees may sit for one, or several, days. Those proposing amendments write to the Revision Committee, and can also appear in person to argue their case—which is normally (but not invariably) more effective than absence. The process is partly self defeating. Writing or speaking to a committee is less daunting than moving an amendment in full Synod. Amendments therefore have multiplied, especially those of the trivial sort. So to be fully effective, members have to devote to the affairs of the Synod not merely the twelve days or so of normal sessions, plus any time needed if they are appointed to boards or councils, but also additional days if they accept any opportunity to serve on revision committees, or to argue their case if they wish to make amendments. Effective lay representation is becoming increasingly reserved for the leisured, the church-employed or the retired. Under the guise of greater lay involvement, effective lay involvement has been decreased.

The point made above that the grass-roots laity tend for a variety of reasons to be under-represented in debate might of course be explained in terms of the reluctance of the elected laity to speak: were it not for another change. In the old Church Assembly, lists of speakers for debates were drawn up on the basis of speakers sending in their names, usually in writing before the session. They were called in order as their names were sent in subject to some adjustment in order to ensure that both sides of the argument were adequately represented, and all Houses had their say. In the Synod names are still sent in, but that is now no guarantee of being called. Members stand, and are called by the Chairman advised by the Secretariat, and less notice is taken of names sent in in advance. Debates are frequently terminated by motions 'that the question be now put' or equivalent: and the members that move such motions are not infrequently asked to do so by the platform. Debates, in short, are stage-managed to a degree that the old Church Assembly would never have permitted. This would be defensible if it resulted in a better balance or a fairer debate. But if it operates in such a manner that certain viewpoints are not heard, or are under-represented in debate, it raises questions as to whether reform has not become a matter of importance, if public confidence in the Synod is to be fostered.

Control of the agenda

The subject matter for debates in the Synod is determined by the Synod agenda: and this is, in theory at least, determined by the Standing Committee. In practice the staff produce a broad outline of the agendas some years in advance, and the detailed agenda is brought to the Standing Committee some weeks before each session. Standing Committee involvement then rarely extends beyond detailed timings, or minor adjustments, with only the occasional addition or deletion of items.

For the duration of the General Synod so far, the agenda has been heavily loaded. I have always harboured a suspicion—which my nicer friends tell me is unworthy—that an over-full agenda has been assiduously fostered. It assists in keeping debates short: it encourages intolerance of minority views which take up time: and it keeps the Synod so busy that it has not too much time to think or to question the platform. It certainly assists in losing from the agenda items like the annual reports of boards and councils to the body to which they are responsible. The idea is also fostered that the agenda is full of items that the Synod has itself asked for. In fact very little of the agenda is made up of items where the first initiative is from the floor of the Synod. The majority of it comes from the boards or councils or from the Secretariat—filtered not very effectively by the Standing Committee. Some indeed may be the result of motions of the Synod: but usually motions proposed by the platform, rather than on the initiative of ordinary members.

I campaigned unsuccessfully on the Standing Committee for the Synod itself to have an opportunity to ballot for which items it should debate, or for the order in which they were taken. As is the way with the Standing Committee, this was diverted into the 'ballot' now held on private members' motions—where the order in which they are dealt with is determined by the number of signatures they attract: but no way did officialdom wish some similar process to be attached to 'official' motions. But why not? There is at present no satisfactory way the Synod can say 'We don't want to discuss that', or 'We would prefer to deal with something else as more important at present' short of a procedural motion such as that 'the question be not now put'. But such a motion stands no chance of success unless the main motion is one on which the Synod has a desire not to express an opinion: it effectively cannot be used to propose that another subject is a better use of Synod time. But until the Synod, in some effective form, takes control of its own agenda, the present frustration of the laity will continue. The obvious way that this should be done is through an effective elected Standing Committee. It should be its business to see that a few important things are done well, and thoroughly, rather than that we attempt too much, and do it badly. Has no one noticed that it is relatively recent Church legislation that has most to be amended? Has no one noticed that Synod pronouncements on social and ethical issues often have almost no impact, because they are too shallow?

The role of 'party' groups

It is often thought that Synod issues are influenced greatly by 'party' organization. This is only true to a limited extent. As far as I am aware three such 'party' organizations exist—the Catholic Group, the Evangelical Group, and the Open Synod Group. All are joint clerical-lay groups, though the Open Synod Group is related to the old 'Non-Party' Group of the Church Assembly, which was for laity only. The Open Synod Group lost some of its cohesiveness with the failure of the Anglican-Methodist Scheme followed by the failure of the Covenanting proposals: they give the impression of favouring change without too much conviction as to the nature of the change required. The Evangelical Group also lost such cohesiveness as it had. Their clergy were anxious to merge with the effective, but unofficial lay group which had existed in Church Assembly days; and merging with it ensured its ineffec-tiveness as some of them propagated the post-Keele desire to 'throw the baby out with the bathwater', and demonstrated their new-found 'liberation' by letting slip much that their predecessors had fought for. Their laity were confused by this: but were not impressed.

Only the Catholic Group has retained a good deal of the cohesiveness which from time to time it shows in a common attitude taken on issues of major concern to them: though, if reports and appearances can be trusted, this cohesiveness is also less than it was. But at one point all the groups are fairly effective: they circulate lists of their members standing for election to the Standing and other Committees, or of those whose candidature they endorse. It is difficult to obtain election other than if endorsed on such a list: though it is doubtful if many—of any group—vote strictly in accordance with their favoured 'party' list.

The Standing Committee

The old Church Assembly elected its Standing Committee (or the elected part of it) by a system where each elector had a number of votes equal to the number of vacancies. Accordingly the 'party' with most votes in a given House tended to get most if not all of the seats. This gave a certain degree of common purpose to the elected portion of the Standing Committee. For many years most of the eight elected clergy were supported by the Catholic Group: and likewise most of the eight elected laity were of the same persuasion. With the slight growth of evangelical laity in the seventies, they gained in representation until at the 1971 election five of the eight laity belonged to the Evangelical Group. However certain evangelical clergy then proposed—and the Synod agreed—that in future, election should be by proportional representation. It was a proposal hard to oppose on principle but it had predictable and not wholly beneficial results. Thereafter the clergy and laity on the Standing Committee would of necessity be split more or less 3–3–2 between the three 'party' groups.

Now the Standing Committee consists of some thirty members. Ten of these comprise the two archbishops, two members elected by the House of Bishops, a Church Estates Commissioner, and five chairmen of the major boards and councils. None of them is elected by the elected members of the Synod. The other twenty consist of two other groups of ten—ten clergy (the two Prolocutors and eight elected by the House of Clergy), and ten laity (the Chairman and

37

Vice-Chairman of the House of Laity and eight elected by that House).

The Standing Committee, as a committee, meets about four times a year under normal circumstances. Most of its business is effectively delegated to a number of sub-committees, the structure of which has varied a little from time to time. One tends to deal with longer-term planning, one with the handling of immediate business (the agenda, timetable and so on), and one with the appointments made by the Standing Committee to boards, councils, Revision Committees and so on. These all meet probably at least for four, and maybe for ten or twelve days in the year. Each member of the Standing Committee tends to serve on one and only one of the sub-committees. In addition to the membership of the Standing Committee, these meetings are all attended also by appropriate members of Church House staff—always at least one to take minutes etc.—and at the other extreme occasionally outnumbering the elected persons present.

I do not know what a trained sociologist would make of the group dynamics of such a committee: I can only make my own observations. In my experience of some twelve years on the Standing Committee its proceedings have been presided over by archbishops acting with invariable discretion. The clergy, however, with certain clear exceptions, show a marked reluctance to oppose anything to which the archbishops have hinted their approval. The laity do not suffer from the same inhibitions. The chairmen of boards and councils tend (understandably but not invariably) to vote together.

In the old Church Assembly days, with the elected clergy and laity in the Standing Committees tending to form a cohesive body with a largely common party sympathy, the balance of power tended to be with the twenty elected members where they made common ground. If they differed, the balance shifted to the non-elected members. With the advent of proportional representation, the elected members tended to divide on most issues, and the balance shifted markedly to the chairmen of boards and councils. The 'vacuum' in positive leadership, which was the direct result of proportional representation, with the elected members cancelling each other out, has had to be filled, possibly not wholly unwillingly, by the Secretariat.

At the outset of synodical government there was an attempt

38

made to get a rather different kind of Standing Committee, where the executive body would have been effectively the chairmen of the boards and councils, and the role of the elected members would have diminished. This the Synod wisely rejected: though, no doubt the same kind of proposal will be raised again in the current review of Synod procedures. But it does raise the question of the relative roles of boards and councils on the one hand and the elected Synod on the other, to which I shall return shortly.

Financial control

At one time the Standing Committee appointed four of the seven members of the Budget Review Group which effectively controlled the Synod Budget—the other three being from the Central Board of Finance (CBF) including its chairman. I served for two years as the chairman of the group. It was a very gentlemanly affair but after the first group of meetings, I was tactfully asked not to ask 'hostile' questions. Since nothing that would have been deemed even remotely 'hostile' in the real world outside had been asked, I found this amusing though symptomatic of the sheltered life of Church House. But, the second year (1977) brought a small crisis. ACCM lost control of what funds would be needed for ordination candidates, and the CBF showed all the signs I associate with panic, and asked for a vote of £1,300,000 for 1978 (compared to £483,000 asked for the year before, which was proving inadequate). Simple arithmetic and logic showed that on the worst possible assumption no more than £1,050,000 could possibly be required, and I indicated reluctance to agree to any more and at length the CBF accepted my figure. (The actual need proved to be about £810,000.) But the then chairman of the CBF, realizing he could have been out-voted, demanded a new committee, of which he would be chairman, and on which the CBF should have the majority: and a craven Standing Committee agreed. Needless to say, the same or similar mistakes were then repeated in the 1983 Budget. It seems to me to illustrate the outwardly gentlemanly face of Church House, which nonetheless takes good care to see that power resides in its own hands. One does not have to work there long to suspect that *Yes Minister* is not so much a comedy show, more a kind of documentary! Financial control, adequate no doubt

39

by Civil Service standards, is now in my opinion inadequate by normal business standards.

The boards and councils

Clearly the boards and councils, and the elected members of Synod, have to work in some kind of partnership. But two views, at the least, exist as to the nature of the partnership. The first argues that the authority to speak in the name of the Church ultimately lies in 'the whole body'—in the bishops and the electorate of the Houses of Clergy and Laity—and that the Synod should therefore appoint to the boards and councils those who have expertise in the fields concerned, and who also have representative views: and should generally oversee the work of those boards. The second argues (from administrative convenience?) that once appointed, the boards contain the representative expertise and should be free to pursue their work with a minimum of interference from the Synod. After all, the expertise in the subjects is in the boards, not on the floor of the Synod.

Both views have a point: and both are intolerable if taken to the extreme. On the one hand, it would be intolerable if, after appointing a board or council, the Synod reviewed and possibly over-ruled every little thing it did: but it would also be intolerable if, once appointed, the board acted on matters of substance in a manner contrary to the clear opinion of the majority of the Synod. Over the years of synodical government, there has been a clear shift—in practice, regardless of theory—from the first view towards the second. It is seen in many ways. Annual reports are now rarely debated—and when they are, the debate comes so late as to be nearly pointless. Financial votes giving or taking a nominal sum in order to express pleasure or displeasure with a Council have been positively discouraged by at least one 'chairman'. Debates on issues touching on the affairs of a board have been discouraged until the board produces a paper setting out its views, as if the Synod had no right to an opinion until it received advice. Boards and councils have increasingly invited Synod members to meetings to propagate the views of the board, as if the Synod was to be an agency of the board, and not the other way round. Recently with the Warnock Commission Report we had the Board of Social Responsibility submitting controversial evidence to the Government in the name of the Church: and not circulating that evidence to the Synod on grounds of expense! Gone, apparently, are the days when reports said they had only the authority of the council concerned, and meant it! It is the writer's belief that the pendulum has swung too far and must be brought back to centre. It is in 'the whole body' that the 'fulness of the Spirit' resides. The Synod must not nag its boards, but the boards do have to treat the Synod seriously. The ultimate human authority lies in the House of Bishops, and in the electorate of the other two Houses, not in the boards. The Synod is there to keep the boards and councils in touch with grass-roots opinions, and not to be educated by or propagandists for the boards. The flow of information between boards and the grass-roots via the Synod members has to be upwards as well as downwards.

The House of Bishops and the Synod

It is not only boards who do not always treat the Synod and its work seriously. The House of Bishops, after the Synod (including the House of Bishops) had voted for Option 'G' in the remarriage debates, made inquiries in their dioceses, and decided not to proceed with that option. Their preferred alternative the diocesan synods rejected. But to whom did they make inquiries? In some, indeed many—but not all—cases the consultation was with the diocesan synod. That was fair enough. But what of the others? Do some bishops not believe that the proctors and lay members of the General Synod, or their diocesan synods represent their clergy and people? If not, why not: and if not who are the people who are more representative, and why did they not tell the General Synod who they were? Why do they seek to by-pass the Synod with their 'Services for Holy Week' when they know quite well many in the Synod will find them unacceptable? And why do they not bestir themselves to see that the clergy do not—as at least a few do—disregard the requirements of the Worship and Doctrine Measure and impose on parishes forms of worship which the parish laity have not agreed to? If synodical government is to work, all have to work together—bishops, clergy and laity working with each other.

41

The record of the Synod

The evidence that synodical government, as at present operated, has largely failed to achieve the standards of the Church of the apostolic age as described by the 1902 Convocation report can be seen by examination of its record of achievement. For instance, if it is 'responsive' to 'the life and action of the whole body', how is it that it produced a book of services which, on account of its complexity, has been called 'the most clericalised in the history of the Anglican Church': self-evidently not what Lord Blanch claimed it to be at the 1980 Synod Inauguration 'a people's book'. If the Synod is responsive to the 'life and action of the whole body', how is it that it approved the setting up of the Crown Appointments Commission without reference to the grass-roots level, from whom it had no mandate? That commission effectively gave a minority say to the laity (the majority of the Church) in Crown Appointments, and set up what is essentially—in spite of all claims to the contrary—a hierarchical system, which the Synod proposes shortly to extend. The harm done to the laity's position in this single piece of retrograde 'reform' is quite intolerable. If the Synod is responsive to the Holy Spirit, given to 'the body as a whole' how is it that it allows doctrinal and moral ambiguity and confusion, a condition which one finds it hard to associate with the Spirit of Truth? If it be asserted that the Synod already achieves those ideals for which it was set up, how is that there is a waning enthusiasm and growing disillusionment in the parishes?

The disease is not yet, and need not be, terminal. Laity in the parishes have to be awakened to the situation, and return to the Synod men and women with real grass-roots experience and a willingness to pull their weight. The weak link of the deanery synods needs to be strengthened. The General Synod needs a strong Standing Committee able to offer real leadership, to restore the balance between boards and Synod, and to reform its structures so as to ensure that the lay voice is adequately heard. Is it too much to hope that the 1985 Synod will see a determined start to this? Only by action along these lines can confidence in the system among the laity be generated. It has not yet been earned. Only by something like this can the trust placed in the Church by Parliament in agreeing to the Synodical Government Measure prove in the end to have been justified.

NOTES

1   *Crucible* (October–December 1976 and April–June 1982).
2   *Report of Proceedings*, vol. xxxiii, No. 1, p. 71.

4

The Need for Revision

D. W. Gundry

In the drama of human life the aesthetic appeal of institutions is basic, because it ministers to deeply felt needs both socially and personally. It is little wonder that a church organized as the Church of England has been re-organized in this century gradually loses adherents. It becomes simply dull and self-contained. Its authority no longer resides in the historic tradition it is supposed to safeguard but in its uncritical assumption that parliamentary democracy is the right form of government for the Church. Nothing could be less attractive as the organ by which human beings keep in touch with the eternal. Happily most people are not concerned with parochial and diocesan administrative structures; as far as religion is concerned, baptism, confirmation, marriage, burial, ministrations in times of crisis and worship at the major festivals still make up 'the dance of life'.

The church activist, however, is more and more drawn away from the mystery and involved in the business of the Church, which tends to become an end in itself. There are even those who spuriously justify the profusion of ecclesiastical administration as a kind of sacramentalism. But in the Church, as elsewhere, administration is best when it is minimal and hardly evident.

Never since the Middle Ages was the Church more highly organized and administered than today; and yet never were there fewer involved in the life and worship of the Church. The baptized are even discounted because they are many. Only those on the electoral roll, a relatively small number, are regarded as the Church.[1] The General Synod seems to be unaware of the plain fact that, as the denominational machinery of the Church of England has increased in this century, so its baptized membership, its numbers of confirmation candidates, its numbers of Christmas and Easter communicants, and even the numbers on its parish electoral rolls have declined.

This is almost relished by some, so far has sectarianism eaten into their souls. A ghetto mentality has become fashionable. Any hint of Christian infusion of culture and institutions or of Christian triumphalism is disapproved of. The Emperor Constantine was a bad thing for Christianity. We should, it is urged, return to the catacombs and welcome the status of a persecuted minority like that of the first and second century. The disengagement of Church and State is openly courted.

But the long-term implications of this are generally missed. There can be no stopping at the catacombs. The logical end is reduction to a handful and then to the lonely crucified Christ, whose latter-day disciples have lost their nerve to conquer. The irony is that there would be no Christian Church today if there had been no Constantine and thereafter no sagacious, persistent, politically adept institution to endure through the Dark Ages and discipline later ages.

On a more immediate, practical level any retreat by the Church from engagement with the nation must imply the eventual alienation of the assets of the Church Commissioners. A shrinking, exclusive sect cannot expect to enjoy the religious endowments of the nation. The General Synod, still in its infancy and with a lot to learn about being in the world and yet not of it, must make up its mind whether it is ready to serve the Church of England as such or prefer the status of a small Anglican sect.

In the latter half of this century the Church of England has undergone an accelerating change in its internal structures and in its relation to the nation at large which calls for urgent re-examination. We have now had fifteen years of experiment in synodical government, but its present shape should not be taken as fixed and final. There are, of course, vested interests in it; but they should not dictate the future of Church of England government. We must not imagine that the first major step in democratization was the setting up of the Church Assembly in 1919, of parochial church councils in 1921 and the still more radical step of the setting up of the General Synod in 1970. These were rather the culmination of a longish process with a decidedly nineteenth-century flavour.

It all began with a meeting of clergymen and laymen from the rural deanery of Akeley at Ashby-de-la-Zouch on 12 October 1848. Synodical government was advocated as the remedy for the

D. W. Gundry

spiritual dereliction of the English Church at that stage. Subsequent meetings up and down the country set up Church Unions
and diocesan synods, later to be enlarged as diocesan conferences.
The demand by a minority for the independence of the Church of
England from the State gnawed away through the rest of that
century and into the twentieth up to the passing of the Enabling
Act.[2]

Not that the revival of the Church of England depended upon
such a trend. It is one of the ironies of its post-Reformation history
that the most creative movements took place during the very
period in which Convocation did not meet effectively, namely from
1717 to 1852. It is tempting to suspect that the Evangelical
Revival, the Oxford Movement and the Broad Church school
would have not been so significant if they had been subject to
synodical control. They might have been more manageable but
they certainly would not have been so powerful. Indeed, one of the
problems of the present General Synod is its inevitable bias
towards compromise and mediocrity. Strong government is hardly
likely from such a democratic assembly whose 'cabinet' (the
standing committee) and whose 'cabinet ministers', also acting as
regional commissioners (the bishops) are a curious kind of permanent coalition.

The fact of the matter is that present-day Church of England
synodical government is fundamentally a Victorian period piece,
born out of time. It apes Parliament and is wedded to the
committee process, yet without those very features which make
political parliamentary government workable. Although parties
exist in the Church and are at times influential behind the scenes
and at the quinquennial synodical elections, there is no party
government and no change of ministers. Some centralization in the
Church is, of course, necessary; and nothing in this essay is
intended to denigrate the permanent officers of the General Synod,
whose civil-service type of devotion and efficiency are unexcep-
tionable. They have no authority to approve of or to change the
system: they are its servants.

The question is whether the existing General Synod is really the
best way of running the Church of England which is so much part
and parcel of England itself and at the same time part of the
historic Catholic Church. Indeed the *ecclesia anglicana* predates
the kingdom of England, and has been historically and institu-

46

tionally bound up in that kingdom ever since it took shape over a thousand years ago.

During the past two centuries, of course, changes in England itself have led to a demand for more self-government in the Church of England. Nonconformity, Roman or Protestant, no longer carries the designation of dissent: we talk of Free Churches, not that they are really any more free than the Church of England. Today there are also several million adherents of non-Christian faiths in our midst, and many would describe themselves as humanist or agnostic. These have all modified the nature of the Church of England itself.

A considerable number in Parliament do not belong to the Church of England. There are, for example, about forty Jewish M.P.s among the 650 members of the House of Commons, and a similar number of Roman Catholics. There are nearly forty Jewish and about seventy Roman Catholic peers. Hence the argument that the Church of England should, in theory at any rate, not be subject to any kind of Parliamentary oversight, even though it now has a large degree of self-government as a result of legislation in this century. The Worship and Doctrine Measure 1974, and the non-statutory agreement in 1976 between the then Prime Minister, Mr James Callaghan, and the Archbishop of Canterbury and Sir Norman Anderson, then chairman of the General Synod House of Laity, on the appointment of bishops were notable steps towards sectarian independence. We are familiar with the argument that further steps should sever the Church-State link completely. What if the Prime Minister were a Roman Catholic or a Protestant Free Churchman or a Jew or of another faith? Why should a multi-religious body like Parliament today have to approve of more important measures drafted by the General Synod? But such simplistic questions miss the very nature of England itself.

In fact the majority of members of the House of Lords and the House of Commons are members of the Church of England; and when it comes to the appointment of bishops the Prime Minister is the servant and adviser of the Sovereign, who is Supreme Governor of the Church of England. Church matters that come before Parliament are scrutinized by the ecclesiastical committee of Parliament which consists of lay members of the Church of England. And it is a very good thing that lay churchmen who are directly involved in national government and legislation and who are free from the parochialism of the General Synod should be guardians of the Church of England as an essential part of England itself. One must also not forget that the Archbishops of Canterbury and York, the Bishops of London, Durham and Winchester and 20 senior diocesan bishops, as lords spiritual, have a voice and vote in Parliament. Add to this the fact that about 27 million of the 47 million citizens of England are baptized members of the Church of England; and it is highly appropriate that there should be an organic relationship between Church and State.

At first sight it may seem strange that Roman Catholics and Free Churchmen generally do not object to this. They prefer to follow their own independency in religious matters; but they know that if the Church of England were to be disestablished, it would not be to their benefit. England would have declared itself areligious. Yet some kind of unofficial ideological establishment there would have to be; and it would be secular and dubiously Christian. Further, Church disestablishment would, unless perhaps the Roman Catholic Church managed to assert itself strongly enough behind the scenes, be one step towards republicanism, which is alien to the English ethos.

One of the depressing features of British national life and even more so of Church life today at a certain level is its anti-historicism. There is an almost undetected but insidious movement to break up the organic wholeness of the nation. This comes not from immigrants and naturalized subjects but from unrepresentative radicals, who have infiltrated the Church itself. The General Synod could usefully examine how far it and, through it, the Church of England officially is being used to further particular political and economic programmes which deliberately seek to uproot English society.

The old quip, 'the Church of England is the Conservative Party at prayer', is certainly no longer true, if indeed it ever was. In the eighteenth and early nineteenth century the older High Anglicanism and the older Toryism went hand in hand; but it has not been the case since. The devout High Anglican Gladstone, 'the greatest Victorian', was the leading nineteenth-century Liberal.[3] Earlier in the present century Labour prime ministers used their ecclesiastical patronage to appoint socialists to high office in the Church, but generally subsequent prime ministers of both dominant parties have avoided political appointment; and it is to the credit of bishops themselves that with very few exceptions they have hidden their personal political adherence. That they have done so was evident from an absurd attempt to expose their political affiliations in a *Daily Express* article of November 1984. Most of them were supposed to be left-wing Tories. It was wide of the mark. Perhaps it was a piece of journalistic mischief to draw the bishops out. If so, it did not succeed. In the House of Lords the bishops are crossbenchers.[4]

It is in the boards, committees and staffing of Church House that political pressure needs watching, particularly when reports on social and economic issues are produced. The incomplete parliamentary pattern of the General Synod becomes evident, because there are only 'members', 'committees' and a 'civil service' but no 'party government' and no 'ministers' in power. Indeed the 'committees' and the 'civil service', and through them individuals with an axe to grind, often give the impression that they are speaking *ex cathedra* for the Church of England.

It is argued that the General Synod can be a forum for debate and a large-scale educational exercise on matters of national and even international concern. But this is often fruitless and occasionally foolish. The Synod is not, and ought not to be, a shadow of Parliament itself, and does not have the necessary expertise at its beck and call. This was all too evident in the much-publicized debate on The Church and the Bomb in 1983 and subsequent discussion on nuclear arms. It has been evident, too, in debates and reports on economic matters and more recently in the emergency debate on the Warnock Report, though on this occasion it was to the credit of the Bishop of Birmingham and the Board for Social Responsibility, supported by the Archbishop of York, that they wanted more thorough and thoughtful discussion on *in vitro* fertilization.

One of the built-in weaknesses of the General Synod is that it sets itself up as an arbiter on questions about which there is national concern, and assumes it can provide a 'Christian' answer. This is arrogant. More importantly, it fails to recognize that there are Christian men and women out in the councils of the nation, including Parliament, who are wrestling with these very things. As one listens to many General Synod debates, one wonders why, if they suppose they are competent to advocate views on political and kindred matters, churchmen in the Synod do not seek a seat in

Parliament or local councils or professional bodies charged with policy and decision-making.

It is as if the relatively few Church activists suppose they alone can speak with a Christian voice. However, it is doubtful whether there is a distinctive Christian political or economic system. There are distinctive theological norms and insights, but these can be claimed by most political parties and economic schools. Even parliamentary democracy is not necessarily the only Christian polity, though it may be the best that charitable men, Christian or otherwise, can agree on as the least unsatisfactory form of secular government.

But the government of the Church is another matter. There are various forms of church government ranging from the authoritarianism of the Latin and Eastern Churches to the narrow democracy of the Protestant denominations. The older of such denominations are today in a weak position, even in decline, to which their introverted committee mentality and lack of permament leadership are contributory factors. The Free Churches, like the Church of Scotland, have become well aware of this situation: their annually elected moderators and presidents are often less influential in the Church world at large than their more permanent general secretaries. It is significant that the more alive, growing sects are less democratic and are dominated by strong leadership, often of a charismatic kind. The weakness here, as in tyrannical secular government, is long-term. The decease or removal of the leader leads to schism or collapse.

Traditionally the Church of England shares the episcopate of the Catholic Church at large; but more recently that episcopal leadership has been eroded by the obsession with democracy and its accompanying bureaucracy. The Church of England has reached a dangerous point at which it must make up its mind whether it develops a modified Free Church style of government by allowing its synodical system to assume the collective *episcope* or it maintains the classical collegial episcopate.

The present form of synodical government is debilitating the Church of England. Not nearly enough critical examination has been made of the philosophy underlying this kind of ecclesiology and its effects. The Church Assembly and then the General Synod naively accepted a kind of ecclesiastical socialism as the appropriate way of organizing the Church today. The essence of such a system is centralization. Private and local enterprise within the Church, always its strength, is now discouraged. The General Synod assumes that it alone speaks for and acts for the Church of England. It is not surprising, therefore, that there is statistical decline, and that vigorous religious enterprise is taking place on the fringes or even outside the Church of England as such.

After fifteen years of experience, it is evident that the present kind of synodism is alien to the Church of England as the church of the English people. The Church of England is still based essentially in the parishes, though the General Synod, its subsidiary synods and its bureaucracy have been busy trying to minimize the power and ministry of the parishes, save as sources of income, substituting the deanery and the diocese, largely abstractions to the ordinary Christian, as the significant units of the Church.

Parishes are now threatened, even decimated, and their incomes pooled in order to provide so-called specialist ministries and increased diocesan officialdom. Yet parishes should not only be made more free but also vigorously encouraged to be the Church in this or that place. A General Synod which was content to be the servant of the parishes would be a boon; but at present both it and the diocesan synods are perilously near to becoming oppressors of the parishes.

So far there appears to be little synodical awareness that the Church today is a voluntary society entirely dependent, apart from the endowments of past generations, on the goodwill and generosity of its local adherents and the local community. One is tempted to suggest that churchmen in a newly developed area should seek to revive the proprietary episcopal chapel rather than engage in and support a new parish utterly under centralized control. This would have the added advantage that the sole central link would be the bishop, who would license the chapel and give it his personal episcopal oversight. Such a suggestion may at first strike the reader as bizarre—but not on reflection. Each bishop in particular might consider what his reaction would be. Our guess is that he would find every possible objection; and he would do so not for any profound reason but because he had almost unawares become the slave of the current kind of synodism. Yet what could be more apostolic or commonsensical than the direct pastoral relationship between the bishop and the local church? All the paraphernalia

51

between the episcopate and the parishes then assumes its proper secondary, even inessential, role.[5]

Nevertheless, a General Synod of some sort there has to be to deal with matters of common concern and to oil the wheels of the Church. But the General Synod is not itself the Church of England, which, one hopes, is far greater and is, in fact, more complex than the narrowly organized denomination of the synodical architects. The Crown, Lords and Commons, the universities, colleges and schools, the cathedrals, private patrons, trusts and societies, as well as parishioners are essentially part and parcel of the Church of England. Yet today there are those who would unchurch them and limit the Church of England to a small association of activists and its entire governance to the General Synod and its subsidiary bodies. If they have their way, the Church of England will shrink further, have a diminishing future and abandon its responsibility to the nation as a whole.

This defeatist outlook has grown up just at a time when the nation needs a comprehensive establishment for the sake of its Christian majority beleagured by alien religions and anti-religious ideologies. Far from losing their nerve, Anglicans should be proud of the uniqueness of the Church of England, particularly of its threefold appeal to the Bible, tradition and reason, set out classically in Richard Hooker's *Laws of Ecclesiastical Polity*.

It is the Church of England's function, without which it has little *raison d'être*, to provide for the daily religious needs of the majority of the realm. This is a big enough task, and should be sufficient to occupy the General Synod. Anything beyond this is largely superfluous. After fifteen years of revolutionary experimentation and restructuring, the time has come to call a halt to continual revision. Yet continual revision there will be if the General Synod sits thrice or even twice annually, in order to justify its existence. Most churchmen are sick and tired of the mania for change. Now that it is approaching adulthood the General Synod should restrict itself to the necessary business of the Church, and avoid assuming an Anglican *magisterium*.

It should be noted in passing that there is a trace of panic abroad, which would put the Christian religion into a synodically made intellectual strait-jacket. This must be watched in the interests of truth. If there is an Anglican *magisterium* it is open-ended and resides in the professional experts—the bishops as the guardians of tradition and corporate wisdom, with the theologians of the Church, certainly not in a popular assembly. More will be said of bishops later.[6]

So far the General Synod has attempted to do too much—to subject the Church to central control intellectually and institutionally, to exercise a collective episcopate, to assume a theological *magisterium* quite divorced from the larger Church Catholic, even absurdly to assume a *magisterium* in ethics, economics and politics, and to preach insufferably to the nation while doing little to engage in practical good works itself.

This was well illustrated by the Bishop of Durham's maiden speech to the General Synod in November 1984 when he attacked the Government's monetarist policy. He naïvely instanced the case of a Sunderland family where, he alleged, poverty was such that two boys had only one pair of shoes between them, though in fact there were ample social service provisions to meet such cases. It was amazing that no one pointed out that this sob story was even more a judgement upon the Church itself; for apparently the Church was unaware of the family in question or, if aware, had done nothing itself to see that the boys were adequately shod. This was a typical example of synodical censoriousness, oblivious of any Church responsibility to do something practically compassionate.

There are today so many instances of how the Church, particularly its General Synod, preaches to others but is itself a castaway. If synodical funds were diverted to enterprises which Christian people could undertake to the benefit of the needy instead of to the production of interminable reports telling others what they should do the Church would gain immeasurably in respect and support.

The time has come for the General Synod to cut itself down to size, to reduce its timetable, expenditure and programme and to urge free enterprise in the advancement of the gospel. It is to the credit of many parishes, congregations, groups and individuals up and down the country that they are doing their own thing; but rarely is a word heard about them at Church House, Westminster.[7]

For some time *stewardship* has been the key word in Church administration. Although this is meant to cover the use of time and talents, it usually amounts to raising money. Like any insitution, however altruistic, the Church cannot live without it. A large proportion of every parish's hard-won income, once a voluntary contribution to Church central expenses, has now become a tax.

Non-payment can lead to punitive penalties, such as the withdrawal of ministry or even church closure. This burden would be considerably eased if the General Synod were seen to be more frugal in its own management or were seen to contribute to answering crying needs which even the so-called Welfare State cannot meet.

One of the outstanding gaps, for example, is the provision of care for the dying and for the elderly and the incapacitated who are not covered by State provision or voluntary societies. There are many other areas where perhaps only the Church can serve the community. Nevertheless these things are not the stuff of the General Synod's agenda. These are left to other Christian agencies; and yet the General Synod presumes to identify and define the whole range of the Church's work and witness.

This kind of ecclesiastical organization is too restricted for the Church of England. It is proving to be a period piece which takes the British parliamentary system with its concomitant civil service and an all-embracing socialist ideology as the model for the life of the Church. The ecclesiastical planners, however, have not had it all their own way: it never dawned on them that such a system implied party government and changing administrations after each election. It is all very well for critics to lament party machinations in the General Synod, as they have done latterly; but such a form of government implies party conflict and, if it is to work in parliamentary style, changes in administration. At that point the synodical structure falls short. The result is a General Synod which is a frustrated democracy.

That it is such springs from the grudging admission that the Church of England is not and should not be a democratic institution after all. Anglicanism is committed to episcopacy. However, democratic pressure has led to a vague notion of a 'constitutional episcopate'. The bishops, like the Crown and the Lords in the secular sphere, are regarded as subject to the will of the popular assembly. This is a modern view, though there is a token acknowledgement of the Church as fully episcopal in the powers accorded to the House of Bishops in matters relating to doctrine and worship.

In practice the bishops have latterly become the servants of the General Synod. Roman Catholic and Orthodox observers are often amazed at this, and wonder how such bishops could fit easily into any reconciled Christendom. The present standing of the Anglican bench is a subject which deserves close examination. The question is whether the Church of England is ceasing to be truly episcopal, save in name. That it is a searching question is evident when Free Churchmen assume that *bishop* means little else than 'moderator' or 'superintendent minister'.[8]

The bishops themselves are so caught up in this development that they hardly know how they stand in relation to the historic threefold order on the one hand and to presbyterianism on the other. As an experienced bishop put it when asked how the Anglican episcopate had changed during his quarter of a century on the bench, 'When I began, the bishop was the authority in his diocese and shared the collegial authority in the Church at large. That authority has now been eroded by the advent of the General Synod. All that is left is pastoral responsibility without authority.' Bishops have become the regional executives of the collective synodical episcopate. This is far removed from the historic episcopate and from the kind of religious leadership that is now desperately needed.

Whatever high views a priest has of the episcopal office when he is called to it, he is soon worn down by the synodical system and becomes conditioned to its demands, except in all too few instances. This conditioning, too, calls for fuller investigation. A book or a doctoral thesis? It is a particularly strange feature of synodical government in the Church of England that the mind of the House of Bishops is so often far removed from the mind of the House of Clergy, as has been clearly shown in voting on several important occasions over the past fifteen years, such as schemes for church union and the ordination of women to the priesthood.[9]

A simple explanation might be that bishops out of their experience in high office gain a wider vision of how the Church should go forward, while the clergy are more concerned to safeguard their own interests by clinging to the status quo. But the variance between the bishops and the inferior clergy can be more surely interpreted quite otherwise. It is the clergy who are much more aware of the Church of England as part of the larger Church: whereas the bishops are soon caught up in the insular synodical system which moulds its own kind of chief executive.

Fortunately this capitulation is not entire. It is to the credit of the present Archbishop of Canterbury that he maintains and is developing his own headquarters at Lambeth, quite distinct from Church House. Several areas, for example Anglican-Roman Catholic conversations, are not within the purview of the General Synod, and can hardly be. Again, when they speak in the House of Lords the bishops speak as such and not as delegates of the General Synod. Even so, they are otherwise dangerously near becoming moderators. The next few decades will be critical; and the bishops would be wise to make a thorough assessment of their role in the Church of England, particularly in view of their closer relationship with their Roman Catholic and Orthodox brethren.

This will not be the first time Anglican bishops have had to ask themselves uncomfortable questions. In his introduction to *Religious Controversies of the Nineteenth Century*, A.O.J. Cockshut wrote:

> The key figure in the history of the church of the first half of the century is not Wilberforce or Simeon or Keble, but the anonymous bishop who, on reading Newman's tract on the Apostolic succession could not tell whether he held the doctrine or not. Nothing could illustrate more clearly the extent to which the Church had lost sight of its intellectual foundations. It was not that the bishops were stupid or uneducated men. It was rather that, taking the everlasting Protestantism of England for granted, and not guessing how soon indifference and wordliness might be replaced by active unbelief, they applied their minds to other questions, and forgot to ask themselves what they were supposed to be.[10]

Today the theological climate and the questions are different, though perhaps not all that different. Today the bishops are pressurized into applying their minds to questions asked by the General Synod, and so still forget 'to ask themselves what they are supposed to be'. They are not only leaders of the Church, as any principal officer is a leader, and, to use the overworked phrase, 'centres of unity', but are historically and doctrinally charged with the government of the Church in a particular place. They may be assisted materially by a body such as the General Synod, but as long as the Church of England is part of Catholic Christendom they are teachers of the faith and guardians of the tradition. One would like to see them initiating more regular fraternal meetings, discussions and co-operation with their fellow bishops on the

Continent and further afield as a corrective to synodical and even ecumenical insularity at home.

However much bishops may shelter behind ecclesiastical democracy, they cannot escape the fact that society sees them, rather than any popular assembly, as the representatives of Christ. Thus, quite as vital as their awareness of their office, is the system of their appointment. In this the whole Church of England, as inextricably bound up with the nation, must be engaged; and the Church of England in this sense means much more than the General Synod. The present bench, so caught up in the synodical machine, may not be altogether aware of how necessary it is that they should stand well above the General Synod and not be simply a constituent of it. Both as bishops of the Universal Church and as lords spiritual in this realm they must reassert their leadership, even if it means putting the General Synod with its bureaucracy in its place. Will they dare? That will show their mettle.

But equally important is the calibre of the episcopate. Whether bishops are competent chairmen and able top executives, whether they are former parish incumbents, whether they are middle-of-the-road men, whether they will go along with current social, economic and political thinking are almost irrelevancies. They must have theological acumen, spiritual insight and a degree of statesmanship, because without those qualities a bishop cannot be an adequate father in God in today's complex society, which now has a global and not simply a national dimension.[11]

The 1976 agreement to set up a Crown Appointments Commission to submit names to the Crown for episcopal appointments was hailed as a step towards liberating the Church from State control. In fact it is tending to place the Church under a narrow sectarian control. The Commission consists of the two Archbishops, one of whom takes the chair according to the province which has the vacant see. Six members, three clerical and three lay, are elected quinquennially by the General Synod.[12] Four members are appointed *ad hoc* by the diocese concerned. The Archbishops' appointments secretary and the Prime Minister's patronage secretary are non-voting members in view of their professional capacity.

So far the Commission is solely concerned with diocesan bishoprics; and after a secret session for each vacancy it submits two names to the Crown. They may or may not be placed in order of preference, though invariably they are. The Crown reserves the right to ask the Commission to submit other names if the two are unacceptable, though this provision has not been exercised as far as is known. In effect appointment by the Crown has thus become perilously near a mere formality.[13] Bishops suffragan are not so chosen: they are nominated to the Crown by the diocesan bishop. At the present time there is some agitation to appropriate all Crown patronage, such as deaneries and some canonries, to the Commission. One member of the General Synod even hoped that the name of the body would be changed from 'Crown Appointments Commission' to 'Church Appointments Commission', such is the deliberate attempt to distance the Crown from the Church.

And therein lies the objection, because such a claim implies that only the General Synod and its subsidiary diocesan synods are competent to speak for the Church, and seeks to disfranchise anyone else. At this stage reversion to the old method of appointment by means of informal consultation between the Crown and the primates seems unlikely; but the Crown, more sensitive to the Church of England at large, should have more than a nominal voice in the appointment of bishops, particularly in view of their membership of the Upper House and their role in national life. It is undesirable that such a limited a body as the General Synod, so capable of manipulation by power groups, should virtually nominate 25 members of the House of Lords.

An improvement would be for the Commission to recommend up to six names to the Crown; but such a suggestion would probably produce a rumpus in the General Synod as it saw its little brief authority diminished. Yet such a modification would have the merit of widening the field and bringing a more adventurous element of variety into episcopal appointments. It might also ensure a better balance of churchmanship across the Church, about which the older system was more careful.

Radicals could retort that the simple answer is to disestablish the Church and exclude bishops from Parliament. This raises an issue which cannot be dealt with here; but the general tenor of this essay has been to defend and commend the Church of England as an essential ingredient of the kingdom of England. Indeed, if ever the Church of England ceased to play that part and became one of several independent religious denominations, there might be little justification for its continued existence, save as a relic from the past or perhaps as an association of middle-ground ecclesiastical liberals who could not find a home in the Free Churches or the Roman Catholic Church.

The advent of synodical government has taken the Church of England rather too far in that direction; and now some reappraisal of the powers and functions of the General Synod is necessary. Eighteen years ago, after a scholarly study of the organizational changes in the Established Church, Professor K. A. Thompson concluded:

> The Church of England has developed a certain degree of autonomy, and is inclined to accept some of the implications of denominational pluralism, but it still prizes its own comprehensiveness and internal diversity, which it preserves by following a *via media* with regard to doctrine, principles of authority, and organization. This is the crucial limiting factor on any development in its organization towards the 'ideal type' of denomination and bureaucracy.[14]

It is this 'ideal type' of denomination and bureaucracy which we have challenged, because, despite an increased element of ethnic and ideological pluralism of recent years, Church and State in England still remain an organic unity, the further disruption of which would diminish, if not wreck, both.

NOTES

1 The baptized membership of the Church of England is about 27 million, of which under $1\frac{1}{2}$ million are registered on parish electoral rolls. As noted earlier, the 250 lay members of the General Synod, however, are not elected by those on electoral rolls but only by members of deanery synods. Exact statistics are unavailable, but a generous estimate would put them at no more than 40,000, hardly an adequate constituency. The 250 clerical members of the 500-strong General Synod are the proctors in convocation, elected by the clergy of each diocese, and a small number of representative suffragan bishops, deans and archdeacons. All the diocesan bishops are members *ex officio*.

2 For a historical outline see Cornish, F. Warre, *The English Church in the Nineteenth Century*, part ii (London 1910), pp. 33f., 42f., 312; Flindall, R. P., ed., *The Church of England 1815–1948* (London 1972), pp. 337ff.; Welsby, P. A., *A History of the Church of England 1945–1980* (Oxford 1984), pp. 146ff.

3 Edwards, D. L., *Christian England*, vol. 3 (London 1984), pp. 219ff.

4   The last bishop to accept the Conservative whip was Dr Headlam, bishop of Gloucester, who retired in 1945. More recently Dr Stockwood, while bishop of Southwark, supported the Labour Party in the Upper House but not latterly. It will be interesting to see whether any bishops formally associate themselves with the SDP-Liberal Alliance, if it becomes more prominent in Parliament.

5   Save that the Church is now so centralized that parishes no longer have control over their own endowments. The central bureaucracy has the whip hand.

6   It is unfortunate that the Convocations of Canterbury and York, as professional bodies, have been run down. The General Synod necessarily leans towards amateurism, content with over-simplified statements on theological and related subjects. It is as if, elsewhere, the British Association had supplanted the Royal Society or the Council for Health Education the Royal Colleges of Physicians and Surgeons.

7   Little encouragement of the missionary and other Church societies is heard in the General Synod: yet they are the active agencies of the Church. King's College London Theological Department, the largest Church faculty for the education of ordinands, was lost to the Church without notice by the General Synod. So, too, was the more recent closure of the choral foundation, St Michael's College, Tenbury. These are illustrations of how the General Synod is interested only in its own departments. It would have been unable to take over these institutions; but its lack of concern was symptomatic of its exclusiveness. The Pastoral Measure has virtually placed all patronage under synodical control.

8   This was clear from Free Church statements when Anglican-Methodist unity and, later, covenanting between the Churches were being debated.

9   Probably no priest is now seriously considered for a bishopric unless he supports the new synodism; and by extension those who oppose strongly lobbied radical causes are unlikely to become diocesan bishops.

10 Cockshut, A. O. J., *Religious Controversies of the Nineteenth Century* (London 1966), p.2.

11 Everywhere the State is bound to have an interest in senior episcopal appointments. When the State is unconcerned the Church will have ceased to be a potent factor in society. In Spain, for example, there is a recognized process of consultation between the Vatican and the Government.

12 There is no mandatory provision for change of personnel: members of the Crown Appointments Commission can be re-elected. Hence the danger of a small caucus of bishop-makers.

13 Mr Callaghan, when prime minister, said he and his successors could not be expected to be mere postmen between the Commission and the Crown. Yet that is what the premier has become.

14 Thompson, K. A., *Bureaucracy and Church Reform* (Oxford 1970), p.243.

5

Change–and Decay

Clifford Longley

Forty or more years ago, *The Times* would announce the appointment of a new bishop to the Church of England by publishing a lengthy interview, recording his views on matters both mighty and humdrum; and sometimes also interviewing his wife. It is instructive to look back through a newspaper's cuttings library, for it illuminates the past and also the present. Today a new bishop, unless he be already a very well-known figure, can expect to rate only a paragraph or two, perhaps a caption to illustrate a photograph. Clearly things have changed considerably; and bishops have to earn their place in the news. That, maybe, is how it should be. The Church is now less central, but also less part of the powers-that-be, less a pillar of the Establishment, free to detach itself from time to time from the mainstream of assumptions and attitudes in order to make well-directed criticisms.

Once he was consecrated and installed, too, a new prelate could expect more generous attention from the media of his day. The cuttings files contain long and respectful reports, often substantially verbatim, usually with little or no analysis or explanation. It was assumed, obviously, that readers were insiders to the Church's affairs, and needed little assistance to understand. And the cuttings also reveal a subtle difference in the style of journalism in other ways. It was enough to report that a leading public figure had 'said' something. The thoughts and the words made the news. Today the emphasis is on action. News reporting is event-orientated, not ideas-orientated. Something said, an expression of a view, has to be turned into something done, a demand, a challenge, a rebuke or an endorsement.

This is the modern world: the mass media helped to create it, but is by no means its only begetter. It reflects opinion more than it leads it. Our institutions too have become action-orientated in the conduct of their affairs; they too feel they are 'doing' something rather than just 'saying' something. 'Actions speak louder than words' is their motto, and so there is collusion between them and the media that report them to cultivate an image of activity rather than of thought. And of course these are seductive illusions arising from this. Chief of these is the siren call of 'relevance' beckoning such institutions as the General Synod away from the ground where they belong and where their real competence lies, urging them to make all the world's affairs their own.

As a national institution, the General Synod has sometimes gained public attention—and deserved it. On occasion, it performs for the nation a service which no other body can achieve, as for instance in the most famous debate of its fifteen years of life, the Church and the Bomb debate of 1983. The issues were of unparallelled importance for the nation, yet there was no other national forum equipped to examine the matter in the light of morality with expertise and wisdom. It was, for once, thought rather than action which counted. The General Synod commands no nuclear submarines, nor was the Government beholden to it for its guidance. But here was the setting in which those who hold passionately to the unilateralist position on moral grounds could present their case as well as they were able, to a sympathetic and informed body which took its responsibilities with the utmost seriousness. They did not win the argument; but they did establish, as had not been properly established before in public life, that the possession of nuclear weapons by Britain was above all a moral choice, not a purely political or military one.

Great was the public attention, too. The debate was televised, and reported as thoroughly as Parliament in the press, with headlines everywhere next day. And it was marked, for once, by a clear understanding that synodsmen are not to be expected to pass judgement on matters about which they know little, such as the niceties of current nuclear strategy in NATO. Because the issues were so grave, perhaps, and because the sense of a responsible burden was so vivid, the Synod kept to its proper business, analysing the morality of the issue itself. It passed a clear judgement on the main question: was Britain's possession of these weapons itself immoral? And that happened to be a question to which everyone in the nation could relate, and needed help in answering.

There were lessons for the General Synod in that exercise, and some of those drawn were not necessarily the right ones. It did not in fact mark a turn in the tide of the Church's influence in the nation, partly no doubt because the solution it proposed, in favour of keeping the weapons but with a 'no first use' condition, was not dramatically at odds with the conventional wisdom. A better test of the Church's influence would have come, had the decision gone the other way. It did not mark the point at which the nation began to look once more to the Church for leadership on matters large and small in other areas. More than once, in the after-glow of the Church and the Bomb debate, the Synod seemed to think it had the opportunity to make a similar impact; yet it failed to do so. One of the chief reasons for the success of that occasion was the fact that the nuclear issue, for or against unilateral nuclear disarmament, was peculiarly suited to the Synod's debating process and decision-making method. It was a relatively rare question which genuinely calls for a yes or no answer, to keep the bomb or not; and not many other questions are like that.

On that occasion it was the Synod's strength. Unfortunately more often it is its weakness. Few questions in morality or theology lend themselves to that binary solution where there are only two answers. The Synod is nevertheless designed to work that way. It is a parliamentary system, modelled on Westminster. All questions brought to the Synod for decision have somehow to be reduced to a formula which can be tested by a yes or no vote. It helps the journalist, perhaps; but whether it helps the church is doubtful.

A recent topic of debate illustrates these disadvantages just as well as the Church and the Bomb debate illustrated the advantages. In February 1985, the General Synod was called upon to make a preliminary judgement on two recent ecumenical reports, that on Baptism, Eucharist and Ministry from the World Council of Churches, and the Final Report of the first Anglican-Roman Catholic International Commission. In the latter case, at the specific request of the Anglican Consultative Council, the Synod was trying to answer three questions. Like all other provincial synods in the Anglican Communion, and in preparation for the Lambeth Conference in 1988, the General Synod was asked to say whether the first two sections of the ARCIC Final Report were consistent with the Anglican faith; and whether the third showed 'sufficient convergence' between the two churches to justify further work in the same direction.

There was a long debate, much of it of good quality. Among the many distinguished contributions, much the most provocative was from the chairman of the House of Laity, Mr Oswald Clark, who is well known for the staunchness of his Anglo-Catholic churchmanship and the scholarship with which he supports it. He declared himself willing to vote in favour of the three motions, but made an erudite and at times fierce statement of dissent from many of the practices and attitudes in the Roman Catholic Church.

It was something of a contrast to the blandness and ecumenical politeness displayed by others. But nowhere in the motions passed (by very large majorities) was there any echo of his reservations, which are surely important for the future of these negotiations. The Anglican Consultative Council will eventually receive the General Synod's final judgement on these matters in the form of 'yes, yes, and yes' to its three questions.

The General Synod does rather tend to assume that there is no other way of going about such business. For once, there was a constructive example soon available of a very interesting alternative way. For parallel with the Anglican world-wide consultation being conducted by the Anglican Consultative Council is a world-wide Roman Catholic consultation, being conducted by the Vatican. Just as every provincial synod in the Anglican Communion is being asked to pass its judgement, so is every episcopal conference in the Roman Catholic Church being asked to respond to those same three questions.

The Roman Catholic bishops of England and Wales published their response to the ARCIC Final Report three months after the preliminary Synod debate. They had started with a lengthy draft, prepared by their theological commission; they had debated it in plenary session several times; they had in fact struggled with it. Their eventual statement also contains, implicitly, the same 'yes, yes, and yes' given by the General Synod. But it also contains some remarkable theology, tellingly expressed, full of useful pointers to the future even including a plea that Anglican Evangelicals should be more closely associated with the venture. Their response was not deemed ready for publication, however, until they were as near as possible to unanimity. In the final vote there was just one abstention. In the process of seeking this consensus, some individual bishops had been carried a considerable distance in their own thinking. There was a real movement of opinion. And it is not premature to say that the English Catholic statement is a historic landmark in relations between the two churches.

It is fair comment—which he did not fail to make—that the Oswald Clarks of the Roman Catholic Church had no forums where their voices could be heard in these deliberations. It was an exclusively episcopal decision. As elsewhere, the English Catholic Church has so far failed to provide for the proper participation of lay people in its affairs. Nevertheless, the comparison between the two processes in the two churches points precisely to the weakness of the Anglican synodical method. It was capable of producing an answer; but failed to produce a full statement. One may ask, and one may doubt, whether there was any real movement of opinion in that Anglican Synod debate; and how many of the Synod members had really faced up to the contents of the ARCIC Final Report. What they thought of Mr Clark's intervention we shall never know. It is far too easy, in the Anglican system, to pass half-hearted resolutions which really imply no commitment. It is impossible, in that system, to produce the sort of reasoned commentary that the Catholic bishops produced. In the Anglican system, it seems, all that matters is the final decision, the yes or no, the 'action' part of the business; the reasoning behind it and all the reservations and constructive suggestions so elegantly presented in debate are allowed to escape through the windows.

To whom, then, are they directed? It is not easy to answer, sometimes. It has become a fairly common experience to see the General Synod embarking on a debate on some contentious matter, for instance issues associated with the ordination of women, when quite evidently a large proportion of the total membership has already made up its mind and is not amenable to argument. Yet the debate goes on, with speech after speech repeating well-rehearsed positions, often with little connection between what one speaker has to say and the next, and no evidence whatever that anyone is actually listening in an open way, ready to be moved from entrenched attitudes. On such occasions it is often only the final vote that matters.

This is all part of the limitation on the General Synod set by its adoption of the parliamentary style of debate and decision making. It is government by majority decision, no doubt a most excellent principle in Parliament itself or in such bodies as trades unions or political parties, where the rule that the majority prevails is accepted by everyone as a condition of taking part in the first place. The Church is not like that; one does not belong or refuse to belong because one likes or dislikes the 'rules of the game'—one belongs for reasons of fundamental conviction and indeed of faith. It is no part of the convictions of an Anglican that crucial decisions touching the life of the Church are to be made by majorities, whether they be 51% majorities or two-thirds. It means, in effect, that there is no incentive in the internal affairs of the General Synod to strive for unanimity or anything near it. The incentive is to persuade the undecided middle ground, if there is one, to cast its vote this way or that. And often the best way to do that is not to seek some understanding with strongly opposing views, but on the contrary to isolate those views by painting them as extreme, so that the middle ground loses sympathy with them. Thus majority rule dictates tactics; and it can reinforce rather than overcome divisions.

But, it is said, at least the principle of majority rule does allow some progress. It is even suggested that those special issues which are required by the Synod's present rules to receive a two-thirds majority should be decided by simple majorities, so that progress would be faster. This is a straightforward appeal to democratic principles: why should a minority be allowed to block the will of the majority? What is lacking, in such arguments as this, is any awareness that majority rule is not some God-given law; it is a convenience, invented by men for men. There is such a thing as the tyranny of the majority and the oppression of minorities; and there is such a thing as the ideology of democracy, which places it as an absolute truth beyond comment or criticism, which only madmen would deny. Yet it needs seriously to be questioned, in matters of church government; and on occasion, abandoned. There is no truth of faith, nor any theological principle, which elevates government by majority above the level of expedient, a useful way of proceeding in certain circumstances. But to put it on one side would be called a recipe for stagnation. It is not necessarily true. It could be a recipe for deeper and more serious debate, and for far greater attention to understanding and meeting the position of one's opponents rather than, as at present, merely out-voting them in the division lobbies. It would force the church to search for its own unity and identity; it would oblige Anglo-Catholics and Evangelicals and Radicals to wrestle with each other's most cherished beliefs, to 'get inside each other's skin'. It would be hard work; but it would be a service to truth, to charity, and to unity. And far from blocking progress, it might even cause it to happen. The Church should be governed by truth, not by majorities; and truth will not emerge when issues are evaded and oppositions out-voted. It is sometimes the minority which refuses to let go of some glimpse of the truth not yet seen by the majority: they need each other, as allies in the search, not as enemies in the battle.

The question to whom do the speech-makers direct themselves is a part of a larger puzzle: to whom does the Synod as a whole direct itself? If an archdeacon makes a speech on unemployment in the course of a debate on that topic, he is, by all appearances, talking to his fellow Synod members. On an issue like that, he may well not be trying to persuade them of opinions they do not already share. He is, perhaps, deepening their understanding of some aspect of the problem. But is it reasonable and fair to ask: to what end, exactly? What real difference does it make if this relatively small selection of members of the Church of England emerge from a debate on unemployment better informed about the details of it? They are under no obligation to take back to their diocesan or deanery synods that particular archdeacon's reflections on the subject, and it is safe bet that none of them will do so. And if all such speeches are added together, and compressed into a resolu-tion which is carried, again it has to be asked: to whom is it directed? And there is a snare waiting to trap the Synod just ahead of such debates and such resolutions, the illusion that something has been done. 'We "did" unemployment two years ago,' as one Synod member put it. There is a confusion of words and actions, as if to say something about a problem was somehow to nudge it towards a solution. And it is in this sort of context that the word *relevant*—a perfectly good word, referring to a perfectly good idea—has been most devalued. For so often it is the words alone, those uttered in speeches and those uttered in resolutions, which have this spurious 'relevance'—there is no relevant action as such to follow them.

This must be, and inevitably is, reflected in the outside world's impressions of the General Synod. It is certainly reflected in the way the mass media react to it. One quite plausible answer to the question to whom does the Synod direct itself may well be 'to the mass media', hoping thereby to reach public opinion in general.

There are occasions, indeed, when that seems to be the only possible answer. Certainly there are on every order paper motions which would not be likely to receive any debate at all, were the Synod meeting in closed session, its conclusions kept secret. And that fact alone seems to confirm that somehow the mass media are being unconsciously recruited by the General Synod for its purposes. It might surprise and shock Synod members to know that the mass media has no such perception of its duty: it is not an arm of the Synod, but representative of the public. It is sad to notice the disappointment, or even a sense of being let down, when some general debate in the Synod receives no press attention at all, even though the motion passed was seen by Synod members to have this magical quality of 'relevance'.

There are distinctions to be made, of course. The General Synod has executive power over some matters; it may command things to happen, and they happen. There is no confusion then between words and actions. But this relates almost wholly to the Church's internal affairs. There is another class of synodical business almost in the same category, when it is specifically responding to a request from outside that it state its view. There may be no consequential action other than the transmission of the view stated; but nevertheless the response has the nature of an action. Rarely, but significantly, the demand for a response is implicit, and arises not from some organized outside source but from general concern in society. That was the case when the Synod debated unilateral nuclear disarmament, and again its response may be seen as having the nature of an action.

But such occasions are graces; they cannot be created by the Synod at will. There is certainly no general appetite in society in general, nor indeed in the Church of England in particular, to know where the Synod stands on all the issues of the day, or even most of them. Yet more attitudes and opinions have been expressed, in the last fifteen years, then ever the public wanted to hear. What a useful and corrective exercise it would be, were the Synod to commission an audit of all its various declarations and demands, over the years, measuring each against the visibility of response. Too many, it would undoubtedly be found, had sunk without trace. But that sort of feedback is not available to the Synod, except occasionally when some desperate member tables a question to ask what happened following some debate and resolution. The answer is almost invariably unimpressive. It would have to be said that there are very few if any significant social changes over the last fifteen years in which the deliberations of the General Synod have had an influence. The most that could be said for it is that it may occasionally have contributed its voice to some opinion already widely shared. On those issues where the Church is necessarily out of step with social trends, the trends have tended to prevail, regardless. There is no better illustration, in the course of the Synod's fifteen years, than its attempt to define some position on divorce which would bear witness to the Church's belief in the permanence of marriage, as a resistance to the growing instability of marriage in society. No resolutions of the Synod had any effect whatsoever; what did have some marginal effect, in the opposite direction, was the Synod's failure to take action in the one area where it could exercise some control, second marriage in church. The long and painful muddle, which ended in futility, only advertised the Synod's impotence and confusion.

These are the penalties for conducting the affairs of the Church in the open. It is a two-edged sword: if the Synod wishes to bask in national attention when it holds excellent and intelligent debates such as that on nuclear weapons, it must run the risk of public impatience or even contempt when things do not go right. What is more, the public accessibility of the Synod is one of the most important and visible signs of the Church of England's continuing status as the national Church. At the national level, it has become the Church's shop-window, where it puts on display its wares for better or for worse. There is no other way. A major share of the Church's total impact on national life is now held by the General Synod, and it has become a key point of the compact between the civil community and the ecclesiastical one. So the Synod is not dispensable; something like it has to exist. And English society in general would be the poorer without it. It may indeed be doubted whether English society would long tolerate an Established Church were its internal workings to be hidden from view. Part of the price of Establishment, therefore, is that the Church has to think aloud, in public—even when its thoughts are muddled, and not going to win it any friends.

Government by majority is not part of the ideal, however. It is not required of the Church that it should marshal its thoughts according to the rules of the Oxford Union debating society. It secularizes the process; and it maintains the fragmentation which is Anglicanism's major disease. A synod organized on such principles rapidly becomes a battle ground between opposing factions, for insistence on the binary yes-or-no result naturally divides the Synod into yes-men and no-men (and women). Its standing orders will prevail over the Holy Spirit, every time.

It was no doubt not the deliberate intention of those who originally designed the Synod's constitution that it should operate in such a way, but that has been the result. And the Church of England is rather alarmingly blind to the dangers. It has become an ideology in the Church, rather like the ideology of democratic majorities referred to before, that its celebrated comprehensiveness is a fact of life and a virtue. Perhaps a virtue it was, when the Elizabethan settlement first began to heal the serious religious differences in the nation caused by the Reformation. The theory of 'one church, many churchmanships' was appropriate for an age in which Anglicanism was truly the natural religion of the English; but that time has passed, and the Church has to adjust to its passing.

The real crisis in the nation is not the old clash between Protestants and Catholics, and the Church is not helped by being structured as if it was. The real crisis is secularism and religious indifference; and it has bitten very deep into the Church's flesh, perhaps mortally so. A comprehensiveness which means several 'little churches' within one big Church is a luxury for which there is no longer any space. For it is not a big church any more. It has the prestige, and it has the money certainly; but where are the members? Its weekly attendance is quite substantially below the weekly attendance of the Roman Catholic Church in England; and if the other Nonconformist churches are added to that, the Church of England's active membership is probably less than half the total of the other churches. A body of such modest size has to face its internal differences with a determination to resolve them; they are no longer grounds for self-congratulation. Yet one of the distinct features of the General Synod in the fifteen years of its existence has been the growth of what is called 'party spirit' rather than its decline. And responsibility for that lies squarely with its constitution and standing orders, which enshrine the principle that all that matters is a 51% majority.

It is quite extraordinary, for instance, that the deep underlying doctrinal differences, present in the Church of England since the Reformation, have been tackled not within that Church at all but in ecumenical conversations with other Churches, especially the Roman Catholic Church. It is there one finds a serious theological attempt to bridge the Catholic and Protestant divide on such issues as priesthood or the doctrine of Holy Communion; and indeed it is there that attempts are being made to bridge the theological divide on 'salvation by faith alone'. These are all internal divisions in the Church of England, but it has made no real effort to overcome them. How ironic it is that the call for greater participation by Anglican Evangelicals in the ecumenical process came not from the General Synod but from the Catholic bishops. Had it been put forward as a motion for Synod debate, the Anglo-Catholic party there would no doubt have voted it down. The virtue of comprehensiveness has become a vice: it means that Anglo-Catholics or Evangelicals or any other group can construct a separate religious identity within the Church of England, and pay almost no heed at all to any other group. Yet this same Church faces a crisis of delining numbers that in the long term will threaten its very survival. And the General Synod not only allows this situation to continue: it is an ideal arena for the party groups to play their games. Indeed, they are bound to do so; the Synod offers no other way forward because of the way it is structured.

Wisdom comes with age, and the Synod has now grown old enough to have discovered that none of the Church's real problems have been solved by tinkering with the inessentials. Not 'relevant' debates in the Synod nor a new prayer book nor any other solution to the marginalization of the Church from society has had a significant impact on this process, and 'nostrums' are now out of fashion.

The vast majority of English people are not now within the Church, enjoying the freedom of religious opinion contained in the notion of comprehensiveness. They are outside the Church, looking in, and wondering what it really stands for. That is perpetuated by the shape of the General Synod, by the public impression of victorious majorities and defeated minorities—'You pays your money and you takes your choice.' What is so desperately needed is a convergence on common ground, and a painful, patient, careful listening to all the diverse theological positions in order that they may become one. But one looks in vain for the sense of urgency in

71

the General Synod or in the Church of England generally, which would tell it that there is a moral crisis in the nation of which the Church's failure is the cause; or that with every possible privilege on its side the Church of England has presided over the de-Christianization of the English people, unable to stop it or even to understand it. Rarely if ever has such a note of alarm been sounded, in fifteen years of synodical business. The nearest to it, sad to report, was the anxious moment at the beginning of the 1980s when inflation was so high that even the vast resources of the Church Commissioners looked threatened. There was, briefly, then, a sense of 'We can't go on like this'. It has not been heard since. One is even tempted to the cynical conclusion that as long as the money holds out, no one is really worried. Not once has the General Synod seriously addressed itself to the issues of secularization and marginalization, or to the continual decline in every statistical index of church life: ordinations, confirmations, baptisms, attendances or electoral roll numbers. Yet in the end this is the General Synod's first responsibility, and if it does not discharge it, it matters little what else it does. The general public knows what is happening. It may even begin to see the Synod as a far-away fantasy world, no longer in touch with reality.

And that, to be personal, is an impression I have had too. To attend the General Synod is to visit an ordered world, but on another planet from 'out there', the life passing by in Great Smith Street, Westminster. It is a pleasant world, certainly; a kind and generous-hearted little island. But there really is a touch of fantasy to it: one feels it in one's bones. If the Synod is to retain its place as a significant national institution, it will have to turn aside from the easier questions and ask itself some hard ones. It needs something, somehow, which will shatter the suffocating complacency of countless illusions and evasions. The Church of England is in deep trouble: it desperately needs a General Synod which can face up to that fact.

6

The General Synod and Authority

Alister McGrath

One of the most vexed questions relating to Anglican theology in general, and to that of the Church of England in particular, is the nature and location of authority. To whom, or to what, should a member of the Church of England look when he requires a definition (either in the sense of a precise statement or a more general limitation of the possibilities) in matters of doctrine or morals? The question is clearly pertinent for those outside the Church of England, as well as those within. The former may wish to know what is required of them if they are to consider joining it, or whether its teachings are compatible with the Church to which they already belong; the latter may wish to know whether there is any point beyond which their beliefs (or lack of beliefs) are incompatible with continued membership. Neither of these positions may be dismissed as 'purely hypothetical', and an inability to provide even a provisional answer to them must be regarded as posing an effective challenge to the identity and integrity of the Church of England. If the Church of England is doctrinally amorphous, and possessed of a theological manoeuvrability which permits practically any doctrinal position to be entertained, subject only to the observance of toleration, the grounds for its continued existence must be sought in the fields of *Kulturgeschichte* or sociology, rather than Christian theology. Such questions raise doubts concerning whether the Church of England may, in fact, be said to have a distinct theological identity in any sense, or whether it merely represents an agglomeration of disparate elements without any underlying principle of cohesion, or even agreement upon the 'fundamentals' of the Christian faith.

There is a growing conviction that there exists within the Church of England a substantial quantity of contradictory opinions and convictions on matters of theological method and doctrine. It has been the merit of Stephen Sykes' *Integrity of*

Anglicanism to draw attention to the absence of any real theological coherence within Anglicanism, exposing the uncritical (and frequently unjustifiable) assumptions underlying much traditional, and some recent, Anglican apologetic. Underlying the question of *what* Anglicans believe is the more fundamental question of the nature of authority within Anglicanism. By what authority do Anglicans legitimate their beliefs, or their latitude of interpretation of beliefs? Of the many vexed questions which the existence of Anglicanism poses, this is probably the most significant theologically.

Perhaps the most satisfactory statement concerning the nature of authority within Anglicanism was drawn up by a committee of bishops for the Lambeth Conference of 1948:

> Authority, as inherited by the Anglican Communion from the undivided Church of the early centuries of the Christian era, is single in that it is derived from a single Divine source, and reflects within itself the richness and historicity of the divine Revelation, the authority of the eternal Father, the incarnate Son, and the life-giving Spirit. It is distributed among Scripture, Tradition, Creeds, the Ministry of the Word and Sacraments, the witness of the saints, and the *consensus fidelium*, which is the continuing experience of the Holy Spirit through His faithful people in the Church. It is thus a dispersed rather than a centralised authority having many elements which combine, interact with, and check each other; these elements together contributing by a process of mutual support, mutual checking and redressing of errors or exaggerations to the many-sided fulness of the authority which Christ has committed to his church.[1]

This concept of a 'dispersed' or 'distributed' authority has come to exercise considerable influence over Anglican self-understanding. It will, however, be evident that this concept of authority involves the preservation of a delicate balance between a number of elements, and the deliberate exclusion of a magisterial authority among them, or in addition to them. Thus the Lambeth Conferences themselves are notable for their studied rejection of any status approaching that of a legislative synod, and a repudiation of the notion of a centralized government for the Anglican communion, which is effectively recognized as a form of pragmatic

federalism. The Committee of Bishops reporting in 1948 continued their analysis of the concept of authority within Anglicanism
as follows:

> This essentially Anglican authority is reflected in our adherence
> to episcopacy as the source and centre of our order, and the Book
> of Common Prayer as the standard of our worship. Liturgy, in
> the sense of the offering and ordering of the public worship of
> God, is the crucible in which these elements of authority are
> fused and unified in the fellowship and power of the Holy
> Spirit.[2]

This emphasis upon the close relationship between the exercise of
authority and public worship anticipates a theme which is becoming increasingly significant in recent theological works—the intimate relationship of doxology and theology, of *lex orandi* and *lex
credendi*—and which develops a very ancient and significant Christian insight into the nature of authority.

The origins of this new trend in contemporary theology may be
traced back to Edmund Schlink's seminal essay of 1953, in which
he argued for the resolution of theological differences through an
appeal to their common basis in the worship of the Church.[3] This
suggestion has proved to be theologically fertile and significant.
Thus Pannenberg drew attention to the importance of doxology in
theology in a significant essay of 1963,[4] and Ebeling subsequently
emphasized the significance of Christian prayer and worship to
systematic theology.[5] A similar recognition of the importance of
worship in relation to theology is also encountered in significant
works published recently in the English language, particularly
those of Geoffrey Wainwright[6] and Stephen Sykes.[7] There is an
increasing tendency to see theology as man's response to God,
bearing witness to his encounter with God as expressed in the
liturgy, and being controlled by the liturgical paradigm.[8] In effect,
this amounts to a rediscovery of the principle *lex orandi, lex
credendi*,[9] first clearly enunciated in the fifth century by Prosper of
Acquitaine, but already clearly in operation during the final stages
of the Arian controversy. The fact that Christ was worshipped and
addressed directly in prayer in early Christian worship inevitably
led to his recognition as being divine, just as the inclusion of the
Holy Spirit in the baptismal liturgy led ultimately to the recognition of the divinity of the Spirit in 381.[10] Similarly, the liturgical

practice of infant baptism proved to be one of Augustine's most devastating arguments for the existence of original sin. The centrality of the death and resurrection of Christ to the faith of the Christian Church are expressed liturgically, particularly in the Sacraments of Baptism and the Eucharist.

This liturgical aspect of authority is particularly associated with, although not restricted to, the Orthodox Church, whose theologians have done much to clarify the liturgical and symbolic basis of episcopal authority. In the early church, the authority of the bishop was inextricably linked with his being the president at both Baptism and Eucharist, the person involved most directly in the enactment of the liturgical symbols which exercise a normative influence over the worshipping community's understanding of the significance of the death and resurrection of their Lord.[11] It is the death and resurrection of Christ which brought the Church into existence, and the most proper response to these mysteries upon which faith is ultimately based is worship and adoration, rather than theological speculation. When faith turns from adoration to seek understanding, it must do so in the light of the precedence of worship over theology. That academic neutrality in theology is the first casualty of this understanding of the nature of theology should not be seen as a demand for a *sacrificium intellectus*, but rather as the response of the believer to God in the light of the paschal mystery, as he attempts to bring his understanding of God, the world and himself into conformity with the symbol set before him. The liturgy of the Church effectively determines the doctrine of the Church. This insight is perhaps best expressed today in the Orthodox understanding of the nature and location of tradition. As Heiler points out, for the Orthodox Church, the liturgical texts are regarded as obligatory norms of faith, preserving the faith of the ancient church, even though they have never been defined as dogma by an ecumenical council.[12]

The *symbolic* understanding of the basis of authority thus rests upon the recognition of the paschal mystery as the criterion by which provisional limits to Christian belief and conduct may be defined. In the early church, the authority of the bishop was linked with his role as the interpreter of the paschal mysteries over which he presided, and in which all shared, passed down to them and hallowed by tradition. The 'story' which is transmitted through the liturgy then serves to stimulate critical theological reflection.[13]

It is, however, an *authoritative* story, in that it limits the options open to those who recognize its authority, excluding certain rival interpretations of the significance of the death and resurrection of Christ, and indicating areas of potential conflict with others. To be a Christian is a corporate, rather than a private, matter, in that it involves entering into a community tradition, expressed liturgically in the story of creation and redemption, by which man both judges his own nature and destiny, and knows himself to be judged.

This insight has long been recognized, not merely by the Church of England, but also by the Anglican Communion at large. The 1662 Book of Common Prayer has consistently been affirmed as establishing the norms of Anglican doctrine and practice by successive Lambeth Conferences.[14] Indeed, some of the bishops attending the Lambeth Conference of 1958 complained that Anglicanism was practically defined with reference to the Prayer Book.[15] By that time, however, the question of liturgical revision was well established, and it was accepted that the 1662 Book of Common Prayer could not be retained unaltered. It will therefore be clear that the renewed recognition of the close inter-relationship between the *lex orandi* and *lex credendi* raises a significant question: who is it who determines the manner in which the Church shall worship? Who is responsible for the revision of the liturgy, with the inevitable doctrinal assumptions which attend such a revision? In the case of the Church of England, the responsibility has fallen to the General Synod. Furthermore, it is clear that the General Synod has discussed and taken decisions upon matters of theology. In what follows, we propose to argue that the General Synod is not competent *de facto*, and should not be permitted *de iure*, to deal with such complex doctrinal matters. In the following section, we shall suggest that, in terms of its *procedures* and *personalities* (i.e., the manner in which Synod debates matters, and those present to debate them), Synod is not competent to deal with matters theological. In the section which follows, we shall discuss reasons for suggesting that, even if Synod were reformed so that these pragmatic objections could be overcome, there would still be serious objections to its having any authority to make explicit or implicit doctrinal statements.

77

I

It is, perhaps, unfair to judge the competence of General Synod in terms of its debates on doctrinal matters. Perhaps it would be fairer to point to its considerable achievements in legal and administrative matters, for which it is well qualified. Nevertheless, the fact remains that the General Synod *does* make doctrinal decisions of some considerable significance, and it is therefore imperative to ask whether it is in any way competent to do so. In the debate on the report of the Doctrine Commission *Believing in the Church*, the present Provost of Southwark (then Dean of Norwich) commented as follows:

> Yes, let this statement be debated by General Synod. I know the excuse. The Synod cannot handle doctrine or has no time for it. But what was the Synod doing when it discussed the Alternative Service Book, or the ordination of women, or heaven help us, the Filioque Clause?[16]

Synod *does* deal with doctrinal matters—but is it competent to do so? How competent are the members of General Synod to deal with the vexed questions of doctrinal development or confessional theology? And does Synod have the time to deal with such vexed questions? The great questions of theological scholarship, upon which so much contemporary doctrinal debate depends, cannot be settled in the pathetically short time allocated for doctrinal debates within Synod's packed agenda. Furthermore, the vast majority of Synod members appear to be theologically uneducated. Why should the Church of England permit doctrinal decisions to be taken by such persons in such a manner? It is significant that the Church of England, having rejected the authority of the Council of Trent, chooses instead to look to its General Synod—yet, as the proceedings of the Council of Trent made abundantly clear, doctrinal decisions were only reached after *months* of continuous theological debate of the highest quality, which commanded respect on account of their inherent excellence and reliability, in addition to whatever authority might be felt to be invested in such an 'ecumenical' council. The General Synod's occasional forays into theological territory, by contrast, make deeply depressing reading. Why, it may reasonably be asked, are there so few competent theologians at Synod? The answer would seem to be that the situation arises through the means by which members of Synod are elected, which make no satisfactory provision for the establishment of a candidate's theological competence. It is, indeed, arguable that no such provision could be made—but that is clearly an argument against Synod's present competence in such matters, not against the principle of ensuring that those who vote on such matters in Synod actually know what they are doing.

There is thus an inevitable tendency for members of Synod to rely upon the theological pronouncements of its sub-committees or working parties, on the grounds that these possess a competence denied to the Synod as a whole, and that they have had the time to discuss the questions at the length which they deserve, with proper reference to documentary evidence. Put crudely—but none the less accurately—there is a tendency to 'leave it to the professionals'. But how reliable are these 'professionals'? Unless the General Synod suddenly became possessed of a theological competence which it clearly does not possess, save in a handful of cases at present, it would not be able to judge whether the recommendations laid before it were in fact to be relied upon. A number of examples from the recent proceedings of Synod could be adduced to call this reliability into question: there is simply not space to discuss them. To illustrate these general points, we may turn to the proceedings of Synod of 13 July 1983, in which the Standing Committee proposed, at very short notice, measures for 'supplemental ordination'[17] for the approval of the Synod.

The difficulty which this proposal was intended to resolve was encountered in the drafting of an Ordinal by which women might be ordained as deacons. How was the problem posed by women who were at present deaconesses to be resolved? Were they actually deacons by another name, or were they something quite different, who required to be ordained *ab initio*? The Working Group dealing with this question initially favoured the concept of 'conditional ordination' (usually thought appropriate when there is some doubt as to the validity of the original administration). This suggestion was put before Synod in November 1982 (on somewhat pragmatic grounds) as the 'middle ground' between those who regarded deaconesses as already belonging to the historic diaconate, and those who preferred ordination *ab initio*, and was endorsed by Synod.[18] However, at their meeting in November 1982, the Working Group—and subsequently the Policy Sub-Committee and the full Standing Committee—were persuaded that the concept of 'supplemental ordination' was more appropriate. The document circulated in advance to members of Synod, however, was phrased in terms of 'conditional ordination', the move to alter this to 'supplemental ordination' being made during the Synod debate itself, in the form of an amendment (proposed at the request of the Working Group and Standing Committee). The member of the working party who instigated this alteration cited Professor John Macquarrie (then Lady Margaret Professor of Theology at the University of Oxford) in support of the suggestion, and made the following case for it.[19]

1 Archbishop Bramhall of Armagh introduced the notion of 'supplemental ordination' in the seventeenth century, thus giving the necessary historical precedent by 'supplying what was formerly lacking in that required by the canons of the Church of England'. This case was cited by the Bishop of Gloucester in a paper to the 1920 Lambeth Conference.

2 A similar precedent was set in the rebaptism controversies of the third century, where schismatic baptism could be 'supplemented' by the laying on of the hands of the bishop.

3 The concept of 'supplemental ordination' was discussed by the Lambeth Conference of 1948, and thence came to be used in the reunion scheme which led to the formation of the Church of North India. In that Synod recognized the ministers of this Church, it thereby already recognized the concept of 'supplemental ordination'.

It will be clear that these three points involved complex details which required examination of documents and weighing of arguments—a process which was totally impossible in the ridiculously short time allocated here, as in general, to matters touching upon doctrine. As the following speaker correctly pointed out, this amounted to 'a major item of theological principle introduced simply by a speech and without proper documents to back it up'.[20] Nevertheless, it was the policy of the Working Group, the Policy Sub-Committee and the full Standing Committee, all of whom might reasonably be expected to demonstrate competence. There would thus have been excellent reasons for members of Synod merely to 'follow the professionals'. The typical member of

General Synod, and particularly the lay member, could be forgiven for failing to have the facts of the Bramhall presbyterian ordinations at his fingertips, or to be familiar with the intricacies of the theology of schismatical baptism. Assuming, however, that Synod committees had given full and careful consideration to such matters, possessing the time and competence to deal with a matter which Synod was being asked to dispose of in a matter of hours, he would hope to rest assured that they knew what they were doing.

Despite the unacceptably short notice of the proposed alteration from 'conditional' to 'supplemental' ordination, these three points were successfully challenged by informed members of Synod, occasionally with facts being cited from memory. The points were successfully challenged as follows:

1   Archbishop Bramhall was merely laying hands upon men who had been ordained presbyters *as an act of conditional ordination*. The act was cited as an instance of 'conditional', not 'supplemental', ordination in the paper by Bishop Gibson of Gloucester for the 1920 Lambeth Conference (which, incidentally, was entitled 'Conditional Ordination').[21]

2   The material referring to the third-century rebaptism controversies related to Baptism, rather than ordination. Furthermore, the third-century controversy concerned the relationship between two separate and distinct ecclesial bodies, whereas the proposed measures were a purely domestic affair within the Church of England.

3   According to one eminent student of liturgy (not, it may be noted, a member of the Synod himself), the Church of North India did *not* employ 'supplemental ordination', the concept by then being 'too discredited to be taken seriously'.

We are not here concerned with the relative merits of 'conditional' or 'supplemental' ordination (although we wish to emphasize that they are very different, and imply quite distinct theologies of orders), or even with the subsequent fate of this proposal within Synod, but with the unacceptable manner in which Synod is expected to deal with theological matters. There can be no doubt that a significant theological statement concerning the nature of the diaconate and the nature of ordination was involved in the Synod's debate on this question. How could the

Synod be expected to reach a decision of such significance, given such short notice and an absence of a critical theological awareness on the part of many of its members? To be dealt with properly, the matter would require full scholarly debate (rather than a highly eclectic appeal on the part of interested parties to absent authorities), and extensive historical inquiry. Theological scholarship must be drunk deeply, rather than sipped, by all those party to theological decision-making. Otherwise, it will simply be assumed that the Church of England does not take its doctrine with any degree of seriousness—and there is simply no room in the Kingdom of God for a Church which cannot justify its origins and continued existence on coherent theological grounds. If the idea of episcopal theological competence by virtue of the charism of the episcopal office is to be abandoned or modified, it cannot be rejected in favour of the totally unwarranted presumption of such competence on the part of Synod members merely by virtue of their election to Synod. In the absence of any proper coherent and generally recognized *theological* foundation for the authority of Synod, the authority of its explicit or implicit theological statements must be judged in terms of the competence demonstrated at each and every stage of their formulation. No Church which takes its doctrine so lightly can expect its continued existence to pass unchallenged from without and within, or its statements to be taken seriously.

II

In the previous section, we were primarily concerned with the pragmatic inability of Synod to deal with matters of theological substance, by virtue of an absence of proper procedures and proper personalities. We are now concerned with more sophisticated arguments which suggest that Synod cannot be permitted to make decisions of a doctrinal nature. Unless a serious threat to the unity of the Church is to arise, the explicit or implicit doctrinal pronouncements of Synod must reflect a general theological consensus. But how is this to be achieved?

The chief difficulty impeding any significant theological consensus at Synod is the absence of any corresponding agreement upon the sources upon which a putative or actual 'Anglican theology' is based. There is a widespread tendency, particularly amongst older

Anglicans, to suppose that Anglican theological method is based upon the 'threefold cord' (Ecclesiastes 4.12) of Scripture, reason and tradition, and that the Anglican position upon any matter of significance may be ascertained by determining whether a given doctrine is consonant with all three. Thus in the Synod debate on whether the phrase 'I absolve you' should be included in the form of service for the reconciliation of a penitent—an excellent example, incidentally, of the intimate relationship between *lex orandi* and *lex credendi*—the discussion at one point hinged upon whether the phrase was consonant with 'Anglican sources of authority—Scripture, reason and tradition'.[22] The failure of this appeal to 'Anglican sources of authority' may be judged on the purely pragmatic ground that those who desired its inclusion and those who desired its exclusion were able to justify their positions with respect to these three criteria. It is, however, necessary to register a serious theological protest against this discredited understanding of the nature of Anglican authority, for the following reasons:

1 The threefold appeal to reason, tradition and Scripture is not characteristic of Anglicanism alone. It is a simple matter to demonstrate that it is as characteristic of the Anglicanism of Richard Hooker or Jeremy Taylor[23] as it is of the Lutheranism of Philip Melanchthon or the Catholicism of Thomas Aquinas. These same sources have been used throughout Christian history, and cannot be regarded as the exclusive preserve of Anglicanism.[24] It is only through seriously misunderstanding the nature of the theological methods of, shall we say, Thomas Aquinas or William of Ockham, or Philip Melanchthon or John Calvin, that this opinion has developed. It is simply not true that Roman Catholicism is based solely upon tradition and Protestantism solely upon Scripture, as Anglican apologists tend to suppose. Arius and Athanasius, Catholic and Protestant, all employ the same three sources in their theological speculation—the difference lies in the manner in which each source is understood, and the significance attached to it.

2 The terms *Scripture, tradition* and *reason* are open to a far greater latitude of interpretation than is generally appreciated to be the case. For example, it is necessary to ask precisely what is meant by the term *reason*. The term is generally used uncritically,

83

particularly by theologians sympathetic to the spirit of the Enlightenment—but what is meant by the term? Are we to understand the term to mean the purely natural human faculty of ratiocination (and thus follow the Deists), or the supernaturally illuminated faculty of reason, whereby man's reason is aided and enlightened through the agency of the Holy Spirit (and thus follow the Cambridge Platonists)? And how are we to take account of the *theological* observation that reason may be subjected to a perverted will, or the *anthropological* observation that man's 'knowledge' is culturally conditioned? Difficulties are also encountered in defining precisely what is meant by *Scripture* and *tradition*.

3 The relative priority of the three sources requires careful consideration. Thus the first period of Anglican theology appears to have regarded Scripture as taking precedence over reason and tradition, whereas in its later period, reason came to be regarded as taking precedence. As the discussion in Synod of the report of the Standing Committee on the Use of Scripture made clear,[25] there was a considerable degree of divergence of opinion on the nature, role and significance of this source of doctrine. While it would be simplistic to state that contemporary Evangelicals regard Scripture as taking precedence over the others, where Catholics regard tradition and Liberals reason to take precedence, there is sufficient truth in the observation to underline the futility of an appeal to the three sources in any matter of doctrine. While there are indeed matters in which the three sources concur (for example, that God exists, and that he is good), as the Enlightenment made abundantly clear, there are areas where reason appears to demand a different conclusion from that of Scripture and tradition (such as the doctrines of original sin or the justification of the *un*godly).

An appeal to the '"Anglican" sources of authority' is thus somewhat premature, to say the least, in that it is merely the first step in a long process of theological debate concerning the identity, nature and priority of sources, which is the necessary prelude to any decision. The somewhat cavalier approach to these sources evident among uncritical protagonists of 'Anglican theology' at Synod and elsewhere renders serious theological debate impossible. It will therefore be clear that the failure of Anglicans to agree upon the precise nature and status of the sources upon which their supposedly distinctive theology is based inevitably leads to a corresponding failure in relation to the substance of that theology itself.[26] This conclusion is certainly true in the wider sphere of Anglican theology, where serious theological debate is a real possibility, and thus further emphasizes the difficulties facing Synod. A serious debate on matters of doctrine would require several equally serious debates upon matters of *prolegomena*—in other words, about sources and methods. Broadly speaking, at least *three* quite distinct, coherent and internally consistent understandings of the sources and methods of theology may be discerned within the Church of England—yet the three are occasionally incompatible. The fact that all three parties (or factions, or traditions) are represented (although not necessarily in such a manner that they may be deemed to be *representative* of the Church of England) in Synod thus raises doubts as to whether Synod can ever achieve a significant doctrinal consensus. If it is to be representative of the present state of doctrinal variation in the Church of England, it can only describe, rather than prescribe. Nevertheless, there are points (in the doctrinal, liturgical and moral fields) where many inside and outside the Church of England look (whether correctly or not) to the Synod for a decision or definition. For example: should members of the Church of England be expected to believe in the physical resurrection of Christ from the dead? As Synod stands, it cannot answer this question, save in terms such as 'Some do, all may, and none must' which are descriptive, rather than prescriptive. The present Archbishop of York particularly commended the following statement from *Believing in the Church* to the Synod in 1982:

> The cement that binds our church together is not a supreme ecclesiastical authority, nor an established confession of faith, not an unshakeable reverence for the decisions of certain councils. It is something difficult to define—a state of mind and an attitude to our religion instilled into us by history. Compromise, tolerance and agreement to differ all play their part in it—and a respect for the individual conscience, a love of freedom, a distrust of authority, a sense of humour, a reluctance to be piously demonstrative, a love of understatement, a hesitation to take ourselves too seriously on the stage of the world, a reticence, a scepticism, a reverence for mystery.[27]

If this statement is taken with the seriousness it deserves, it clearly implies that members of the Church of England are at liberty to dissent from any explicit or implicit doctrinal statements which the General Synod may care to make. We cite the statement here, however, to lead into our discussion of the general problem of authority within Anglicanism.

The concept of authority widely accepted within Anglican circles is that of a *dispersed* authority, located at various levels (such as Scripture, tradition, the creeds and the *consensus fidelium*). Although the decisions of ecumenical councils up to AD 451 are to be revered, those of later councils may be passed over. It will therefore be clear, as we indicated earlier, that it is a delicately balanced understanding of authority, with a number of elements which mutually interact to prevent distortions. There is simply no room within this concept of dispersed authority for a centralized legislative authority such as the General Synod, either in addition to the previously recognized elements of authority, or as their interpreter. The Anglican Communion simply does not possess an ecclesiology which permits a local synod (for that is what the General Synod is) to be endowed with such an authority. It is, however, clear the Canon Law does give a certain legal status to the Synod's *lex orandi* (i.e., in its liturgical decisions) and thence to the *lex credendi*. It therefore cannot be evaded, that the General Synod does possess implicit legislative doctrinal authority—an authority which, as we have emphasized, is not adequately theologically grounded *de iure*.

As studies of the development of synodical government within the Church of England have made clear,[28] its origins must be considered to be *sociological* rather than *theological*. General Synod is modelled on Parliament—note the media's tendency to refer to the Synod as 'the Church of England's parliament'—and the representative principle. Where Synod is engaged in general legislation, this principle appears to be successful, ensuring that authority within the Church of England is exercised in a responsive and collective manner in this sphere. The legislative nature of the body makes a large membership inevitable, in view of the fact that it must be seen to represent its constituents.[29] When the Synod is obliged to act as a consultative forum for doctrinal or ethical debates, however, the principle of representation must be called into question.

86

On what basis may theological matters be settled *by votes*, given the inchoate ecclesiology which appears to underlie much Anglican thinking on General Synod? It was this question which so greatly hindered the formation of the Church Assembly earlier this century, and which was eventually resolved only by the distinction between spiritual and non-spiritual matters. Clause 14 laid down that any measure which touched upon the doctrine or practice of the church had to be accepted or rejected in the terms proposed by the House of Bishops, and that it did not belong to the functions of the Assembly to define doctrine. However, even as early as 1922, there was a feeling that the proceedings of the Assembly encroached upon the spiritual authority of Convocation.[30] As a survey of the *Report of Proceedings* over the past ten years indicates, the General Synod has been unable to avoid discussing and voting on matters of doctrine, whether implicitly or explicitly stated, particularly in the process of liturgical revision. But what are the members of Synod 'representing' when they vote? The simple answer would, of course, be the *consensus fidelium*.

Simple answers are, however, seductive. The authority of the early ecumenical councils is, of course, traditionally held by many Anglicans to be dependent upon the *consensus fidelium*. Thus the committee of the 1948 Lambeth Conference, to which we have already referred, stated this as follows:

> The authority of doctrinal formulations, by the General Councils or otherwise, rests at least in part upon their acceptance by the whole body of the faithful, though the weight of this *consensus* 'does not depend upon mere numbers or on the extension of a belief at any one time, but on continuance through the ages, and the extent to which this *consensus* is genuinely free'.[31]

This view is similar to that of the Orthodox Church on the matter. Thus the encyclical letter of the Oriental Patriarchs of 1848 declared that 'the guardian of piety and faith is the people of the church as a whole'. This does not, however, mean that the *consensus* is established by a democratic vote, but rather that a correct conciliar or magisterial definition is subsequently endorsed by the people as a whole. In other words, the decisions of councils are only authoritative in so far as they are received by the whole body of the church.[32] A doctrine defined by a council is not regarded as a dogma until it has attained the *consensus ecclesiae*.[33] Thus Orthodoxy feels able to reject the decisions of a supposedly ecumenical council (e.g., the infamous 'Robber Synod' of 449). Similarly, twentieth-century Catholic theology has begun to recover an awareness of the doctrine of the *consensus ecclesiae*, which appears to have been totally ignored during the eighteenth and nineteenth centuries. With these points in mind, how can doctrinal matters be determined by the General Synod through a vote? This procedure appears to confuse policy with theology. Synod may well be admirably qualified to determine the former, but it cannot be regarded as competent to determine the latter. More significantly, the consensus in question is not a compromise between entrenched positions, worked out in order to achieve a numerical majority in an otherwise close vote, but a genuine consensus which is achieved and tested over a substantial period of time.

Perhaps most important, however, is the increased interest within many areas of the Christian Church in older models of authority. There is evidence of an increasing reaction against a judicial model of authority (e.g., authority as 'power' or, with diocesan quotas in mind, 'no taxation without representation') and renewed interest in the older models of authority which are based upon a 'symbolic' understanding of the concept. As Nicholas Lash points out, it is inevitable that a conflict will arise between two different models of authority if they are employed simultaneously and uncritically.[34] In the early part of this essay, we drew attention to the model of authority based upon the church as a worshipping community which recognized an authoritative symbol in the paschal mysteries, and a derivative authority in the bishop as the eucharistic president to interpret that authority in matters of doctrine and practice. The new emphasis within Catholicism upon sacerdotal authority as an authority arising within the community, rather than an abstract notion in itself, is particularly significant here. It is impossible to relate this symbolic model of authority to the General Synod, which appears to operate on a quite distinct (if ultimately ill-defined) model of authority. The Anglican pattern of liturgical experience implicitly, if imperfectly, embodies a 'symbolic' model of authority, remarkably close to that of the early church, which calls other models of authority into question. On the 'symbolic' model of authority, the General Synod's right to make decisions relating to the liturgy would have to be challenged, in that Synod cannot easily be related to the Church as a worshipping community. While conceding that every model is imperfect and requires supplementation, the fact remains that the model of authority embodied in General Synod contradicts, rather than supplements, the 'symbolic' model given to Christians upon which they structure their corporate experience of worship and prayer. Sociologists have often drawn attention to the fact that there are several models of authority simultaneously in operation within the Church of England on account of unresolved questions concerning the relationship between the episcopacy, convocation and General Synod: here, we wish to draw attention to a fundamental difficulty relating to the nature of authority itself. What *model* of authority is appropriate for the Church of England? It seems that the rise of synodical government within the Church of England has led to centralized authority and representative legislature in areas where, traditionally, a dispersed authority has been recognized. While fully conceding the need for procedures to deal with questions of canonical regularity and an authority to enforce them where necessary, we wish to emphasize that the crucial underlying question concerning the nature of authority within the church appears to have been resolved by default in favour of a secular model ill-suited for some of the tasks laid upon it. On the 'symbolical' model, the bishop remains the locus of *episcope* within the church.

It may, of course, be objected that there remain no safeguards which prevent the bishop from exercising an authority *over* the Church, rather than an authority *within* the Church. On the 'symbolic' understanding of authority, in fact, the bishop cannot really exercise authority outside the context of the enactment of the liturgical symbol itself. However, the rediscovery of the older vision of the Church was one of the major doctrinal achievements of Vatican II. Thus article 28 of the *Constitution on the Liturgy* emphasizes that it is the whole Church, and not just the president, who celebrates the eucharist. As Lash put this, 'A celebration of the eucharist conducted according to the principle laid down in article 28 should no longer have an individual agent, with attendants and audience. The model is now closer to that of an orchestra, or a public meeting with a presiding officer.'[35] Thus the bishop is not seen as speaking or teaching authoritatively in isolation from the worshipping community, but as part of that community. With these important insights into the nature of episcopal authority regained, much of the old objections to its exercise disappear. Is there not a case for a similar re-evaluation of the office of bishop within the Church of England, which might go some considerable way towards removing the objections to episcopal authority which, in part, underlie the present existence of the General Synod? Perhaps the most neat theological way of dealing with the anomalies of authority posed by the existence and activities of Synod is to revise the concept of episcopal authority, with a view to eliminating the necessity of such a synod in the first place. We have much to learn from Vatican II and Orthodoxy, who seem to have resisted social pressures in order to get their theology right. The success of both Churches in England recently must surely give added pragmatic significance to their understanding of the nature of authority.

It is therefore significant that the church reforms of the nineteenth century, which led ultimately to the establishment of the General Synod *via* the Church Assembly, were not based on any single theological principle, nor even a coherently stated *set* of theological principles, but upon principles of social utility arising from the close connection generally perceived to exist between the Church and State. Thus Bishop Blomfield and Robert Peel, the chief architects of the reforms which gave the Church a new centralized administrative agency in the Ecclesiastical Commissioners, appear to have justified the move solely with reference to the Church's temporal goals and the use of utilitarian criteria. There was no cohesive theological principle underlying the various moves for reform, which generally proceeded upon an *ad hoc* basis with conflicting models of legitimation. As one perceptive sociological commentator has noted:

> On the whole, it was not the espousal of any theory of organisation, theological principle, or political doctrine, which determined the shape of the central church government as it grew up in the second half of the nineteenth century, but rather the conflict of values and interests within the Church, and between the Church and its critics outside.[36]

Perhaps the time has come for a re-evaluation of the exercise of authority within the Church of England, rather than permitting the present situation to continue merely through the cumulative force of accumulated (unsatisfactory) precedents.

III

In the present essay, we have expressed serious misgivings concerning the competence, *de facto* and *de iure*, of the General Synod to take decisions relating to matters of doctrine. These matters are too important—at least in the opinion of the present writer—to be permitted to be handled in this unsatisfactory manner. It may, of course, be objected that the present essay is overstating the importance of these matters. After all, it may be pointed out, most members of the Church of England pay little attention to the decisions of Synod (members of Synod itself, of course, tending to pay more attention). Most Anglicans pay no attention to Synod's more theological pronouncements, preferring to base their theology upon writers (such as C. S. Lewis, Arthur Michael Ramsey or David Watson) who have established their reputations through something much closer to the *consensus fidelium* than Synod can ever achieve. Furthermore, Anglicans will feel themselves free to disagree with Synod where they dispute its decisions on the basis of their own understandings of the sources and methods of Christian theology, and are unlikely to feel intimidated by the somewhat lightweight theological artillery which Synod can muster in response. For example, the contemporary Evangelical—and the present writer includes himself among their number—will continue to work on the basis of a theology of the Word of God, while recognizing its difficulties, and will continue to appeal to the wisdom of Article VI of the Thirty-Nine Articles as an endorsement of the 'Anglicanism' of his position. Should Synod apparently contradict Scripture—for example, by recognizing such a latitude of interpretation of the resurrection of Christ as to include the deliberate theft of the body from the tomb by the disciples—he will feel at liberty to disregard or contradict Synod on this point (and will almost certainly treat every subsequent synodical pronouncement with suspicion—and be justified in doing so). Still further, the canonical enforcement of such decisions by legal proceedings is unthinkable. Why, then, worry about the decisions of such a body when they are treated with such widespread indifference?

For the present writer, the question at issue is the integrity of the Church to which he belongs, which continually appears incapable of theological self-legitimation. As the development of Anglican self-understanding, particularly in the significant statements of the 1948 Lambeth Conference, indicates, synodical government is not of the *esse* of the Church, and, on the basis of the pragmatic criteria available, does not even appear to be of the *bene esse* of the Church. The new awareness of the corporate nature of worship arising from Vatican II, the rediscovery within recent systematic theology of the intimacy of the relationship between doxology and doctrine, the recovery of the ancient and fertile concept of 'symbolic' authority—all combine to make possible a new understanding of *episcope* which strengthens, rather than contradicts, the older Anglican understanding of authority,[37] expressed thus by the bishops of the 1948 Lambeth Conference: 'This essentially Anglican authority is reflected in our adherence to episcopacy as the source and centre of our order, and the Book of Common Prayer as the standard of our worship.' The recognition of the intimate link between the authority of the bishop (or his delegate) and his role as liturgist makes possible an understanding of authority which retains much of the historically Anglican approach to episcopal authority, while employing a model of authority which is not called into question, but is actually endorsed, by the corporate worship and prayer of the church.

Even if the reader feels that these are extravagant suggestions, he is invited to consider whether a body such as the General Synod, which has neither the time, the procedures nor the people for serious and responsible theological debate, should be permitted to make explicit or implicit doctrinal statements—even in a Church which appears unwilling to take its doctrine seriously.

NOTES

1 *The Lambeth Conference 1948* (London 1948), pp. 84–5.
2 ibid., p. 85.
3 Schlink, E., 'Die Struktur der dogmatischen Aussage als ökumenisches Problem' (*Kerygma und Dogma*, 3, 1957), pp. 251–306.
4 Pannenberg, W., 'Analogie und Doxologie', in Joest, W., and Pannenberg, W., ed., *Dogma und Denkstrukturen* (Göttingen 1963), pp. 96–115.

5 Ebeling, G., 'Die Notwendigkeit des christlichen Gottesdienstes' (*Zeitschrift für Theologie und Kirche*, 67, 1970), pp. 232–49.

6 Wainwright, G., *Doxology* (New York 1980).

7 Sykes, S. W., *The Identity of Christianity* (London 1984).

8 Krahe, M.-J., '"Psalmen, Hymnen und Lieder, wie der Geist sich eingibt". Doxologie als Ursprung und Ziel aller Theologie', in *Liturgie und Dichtung: Ein interdisziplinäres Kompendium* (2 vols: Sankt Ottilien 1983) vol. 2, pp. 921–57.

9 See Federer, K., *Liturgie und Glaube: Eine theologie-geschichtliche Untersuchung* (Fribourg 1950).

10 Wiles, M. F., *The Making of Christian Doctrine* (Cambridge 1967) pp. 62–93.

11 See the useful essay of Williams, Rowan, 'Authority and the Bishop in the Church', in Santer, M., ed., *Their Lord and Ours: Approaches to Authority, Community and the Unity of the Church* (London 1982), pp. 90–112. The bishop in question was, of course, at liberty to appoint a delegate to represent him as the eucharistic president.

12 Heiler, F., *Urkirche und Ostkirche* (Munich 1937), p. 190. It is significant that several Eastern liturgies (such as those of St Mark or St Basil) refer to praise as *theologia* rather than *doxologia*: see Hänggi, A., and Pahl, I., ed., *Prex Eucharistica* (Fribourg 1968), pp. 110–234.

13 For a perceptive modern statement of this insight, see Ritschl, Dietrich, '"Story" als Rohmateriel der Theologie' (*Theologische Existenz heute*, 192, Munich 1976), pp. 7–41.

14 e.g., Lambeth 1920, resolution 36 (see *Conference of Bishops of the Anglican Communion* (London 1920), p. 36) More recently, see the perceptive study of de Mendieta, E. A., *Anglican Vision* (London 1971), p. 56, where the identity of Anglicanism is located in the field of 'common and public worship', rather than of 'explicit and clearly defined dogma'.

15 *The Lambeth Conference 1958* (London 1958), Part 2, p. 79.

16 18 February 1982; *Report of Proceedings* 13/1, p. 193.

17 Reports GS 580 and 580A. For the debate, see *Report of Proceedings* 14/2, pp. 620–43, 783–94.

18 Report GS 549; see *Report of Proceedings* 13/3, pp. 919–51.

19 *Report of Proceedings* 14/2, pp. 630–4.

20 ibid., p. 634.

21 For the text of Bramhall's Letters of Orders, see *Conference of Bishops*, p. 155.

22 8 February 1983; *Report of Proceedings* 14/1, pp. 60–1; 66–9. The Dean of Worcester's paper on the nature of sources of Anglican authority, referred to by the first speaker, is not reproduced in this *Report*.

23 The most widely-cited study of Anglican theological method remains McAdoo, H. R., *The Spirit of Anglicanism* (London 1965).

24 We venture to mention our study of the development of theological method from 1500–1800, in Avis, P. D. L., ed., *The Science of Theology* (forthcoming).

25 6 July 1982; *Report of Proceedings* 13/2, pp. 402–26. It is interesting to compare this report with theologically much more perceptive *Constitution on Divine Revelation* of Vatican II.

26 For an excellent critique of the concept of 'Anglican theological method' see Sykes, Stephen, *The Integrity of Anglicanism* (London 1979), pp. 63–75.

27 *Believing in the Church* (London 1981), p. 234; cf. *Report of Proceedings* 13/1, p. 183.

28 See Thompson, K. A., *Bureaucracy and Church Reform: The Organisational Response of the Church of England to Social Change 1800–1965* (Oxford 1970), especially pp. 212–37.

29 Hence the complaints concerning the 'present grossly anomalous situations' in relation to the representation of the laity: 14 November 1984; Report of Proceedings 15/3, p. 1077.

30 See Thompson, op. cit., pp. 182–4.

31 *The Lambeth Conference 1948*, p. 85.

32 See Evdokimov, P., *L'Orthodoxie* (Neuchâtel-Paris 1959), pp. 158–9.

33 See Seraphim, Metropolitan, *Die Ostkirche* (Stuttgart 1950), p. 33. See also Mélia, E., 'An Orthodox Point of View on the Problem of Authority in the Church', in Todd, J. M., ed., *Problems of Authority* (London 1962), pp. 104–16.

34 Lash, Nicholas, *Voices of Authority* (London 1976), pp. 43–54.

35 ibid., p. 45.

36 Thompson, op. cit., p. 126. The sociological distinction between an 'ecclesia' and a 'sect' is significant here, as the former must be regarded as a 'coalition of diverse principles of authority and doctrine' (see pp. 212–43).

37 See Gassmann, G., *Das historische Bischofsamt und die Einheit der Kirche in der neueren anglikanischen Theologie* (Göttingen 1964).

7

Christian Decision-Making

Graham Leonard

Making decisions is an essential function of human life which reflects man's ability to base his actions deliberately upon the consideration of what is true, good and right. It is an activity which he performs both as an individual and as a member of society. Both the areas in which decisions are made and the extent of the effects which they have cover the whole range of human life. What may appear to be a decision in a purely personal matter, such as the choice of consumer goods, can both reflect a particular belief about priorities in human life and a particular attitude towards other people and society in general. Similarly, taking part in the corporate decision of a group or corporate body can have far-reaching implications for the personal lives and decisions of those taking part.

What has been said so far applies to Christians by virtue of the fact that they are human beings but it does so in a particular and distinctive way. Christians are called upon to base their responsible actions upon the nature and purpose of God as he has revealed himself in his activity both as Creator and Redeemer of man and of the universe. Christians are not merely called upon to reflect the content of such revelations and to make cerebral judgements about what is the most appropriate or sensible decision to make. Underlying all Christian decisions there must be a prior commitment of obedience to the will of God. Obedience is both an integral part of Christian decision-making and a necessary ingredient if the will of God is to be discerned. So St Paul says at the beginning of the twelfth chapter of his letter to the Christians at Rome, having expounded the Christian gospel:

Therefore, my brothers, I implore you by God's mercy to offer your very selves to him: a living sacrifice, dedicated and fit for his acceptance, for such is the worship, which you, as rational creatures, should offer. Adapt yourselves no longer to the pattern of this present world, but let your minds be remade and your whole nature thus transformed. Then you will be able to discern the will of God, and to know what is good, acceptable, and perfect.[1]

Here, as elsewhere, St Paul is concerned to make it clear that the way in which a Christian decides and behaves is, or should be, derived from the doctrinal content of the gospel and that if it is misunderstood or distorted the effect will be evident in decisions and behaviour. He also emphasizes that the implications of the gospel will not be discerned rightly unless its understanding is approached in a spirit of obedience.

What has been said applies to every aspect of the Christian life, both individual and corporate, and at all levels. Consideration of Christian decision-making ideally demands a survey of the whole range of the way in which the Church has sought to express and define the content of the gospel, and of the relationship of that process to the liturgical and spiritual life of the Church and to its moral thinking. It is necessary, therefore, to indicate that for the purposes of a short chapter, consideration of the subject has been limited. While much of what is said, is, it is to be hoped, of general application to the Christian Church at large, the immediate issue under discussion is the present situation in the Church of England, and that under these heads. First, there is the general debate on the doctrine of the Church of England and the relationship between public statements of belief, particularly by its leaders, and the formularies to which the Church of England is committed. Secondly, there is, or should be, a debate on how the Church of England should respond to questions of belief raised by ecumenical discussions and how such response should be made. This issue has become acute because, for example, the World Council of Churches has asked all Churches to consider the report, 'Baptism, Eucharist and Ministry', and to declare formally how far its contents reflect its own professed tradition. A similar situation arises in the case of the report of the Anglican-Roman Catholic International Commission. This issue leads to the third, which is the new situation regarding the definition of doctrine which has arisen following the establishment of synodical government and the passing of the Worship and Doctrine Measure in 1974. It must be questioned whether either the Church or Parliament has appreciated the profound change which then took place, substantially altering the traditional position of the Church of England with regard to faith and order, a change which may well put intolerable pressure on its integrity and its existence as a single body.

It is , however, first necessary to consider the whole problem in a wider setting and to discuss the relationship between the Church on earth as a body committed to particular beliefs and its apprehension and expression of those beliefs.

From the day of Pentecost until the consummation of all things at the end of the ages, that part of the Christian Church which exists on earth has to face the problem of how to make decisions. It has to do so because of its very nature and if it attempts to find ways of making decisions which deny that there is a problem and that decisions can be made which are self-evidently right, it will have been false to its nature. This situation arises for three reasons.

In the first place the Church owes its origin to and is given its purpose by the revelation that God has given of himself. The second reason is because membership of the Church is given by God out of his love and is neither the reward for good behaviour nor the result of mastering a technique which qualifies for membership.

As a result the Church on earth is a very mixed society. It is composed at one and the same time of those who have progressed far in their response to the love of God, and of those who have just come to accept it and have far to go in realizing its implications. The great majority of members of the Church fall into neither category. While they have responded to God's revelation of himself their response follows an uneven course and shows a pattern of penitence and restoration. At any one moment because of sin or of an unwillingness to accept the demands of discipleship their understanding of the revelation is imperfect. The third reason is that the Church is a corporate body, a living organism with a common life in which each member is dependent on the others and in which each must be free to exercise the freedom which God has given its members to enable them to grow in their response to him.

How do these basic facts about the nature of the Church affect its capacity to make decisions? The fact that the belief of the Church, its *raison d'être*, is revealed and not discovered by the unaided efforts of man means that on earth it is always attempting to live out a mystery which is beyond its comprehension and by which it should always be ready to be grasped. In this sense, the Church in one respect is in the same position as man, when he seeks to understand the reality into which he is born and upon which he is dependent for life. One of the earliest and hardest lessons which man has to learn is that the world has a structure and a pattern which exists independently of himself and which he can disregard only at his peril. He has to learn that to modify his environment whether for the benefit of mankind or for his own profit by exploitation, is only possible if he respects its structure and pattern and bases his efforts upon it.

If he attempts to behave as if it were what he wants it to be and not what it is, say by defying the law of gravity, the result is disastrous. So it is that any scientist has to base his work upon the facts which he observes while recognizing that any theory which he embraces to explain them has but a provisional quality about it and will have to be qualified or even abandoned in the light of further facts which are discovered, or by a deeper understanding of the facts as they are known to exist. For the scientist what is vital is the acceptance of the necessity for his ideas, his theories, to be for ever at the bar of facts which, though observed by him, exist outside him and are independent of him. This does not mean that he cannot exercise his creative imagination. On the contrary that is the basis of all scientific research. It is often assumed that facts create their own meaning, but as Sir Karl Popper in particular has shown, this is not the case. The selection of facts which are to be observed depends upon the intuitive vision of the scientist as to what the pattern of behaviour might be which is then tested by the facts which he observes often as a result of improved methods of observations.

As a result it is never possible in the scientific sphere to make a decision that this or that theory is 100% true. Its correctness as an explanation or reality is tested by continued application of the theory which will then reveal any defects. It is because scientific theories are in the nature of responses to reality that it is never possible to decide that a particular theory is wholly true by the exercise of some authority whether individual or corporate. Scientific theories come to be accepted as true explanations of the facts by the emergence of a common mind among scientists, not altogether unlike the *consensus fidelium* or common mind of the faithful in the Church.

How does the scientific process compare with that of the Church in seeking to expound the facts which brought it into existence and by which it lives? The first and most obvious similarity is that in so far as the Church believes those facts to reveal the nature of God and his purpose for creation and for mankind, its attempts to express that meaning will always be inadequate and have a provisional nature. To say that is in no way to question the reality of the facts or their authority. It is simply to recognize and accept that their meaning is so deep and rich that the human mind cannot express it fully. What matters is whether the attempts of the Church to expound and explain that meaning are seen in terms of a response to the initiative of God who reveals himself so that man may enter into a personal and eternal relationship to him rather than in terms of man trying to decide what is reasonable and acceptable for him to believe.

The second similarity concerns the necessity and nature of tradition. No scientist can work creatively without entering into the scientific tradition though he will test and seek to develop it by his own observation and interpretation of the facts. The scientist who tried to start from the beginning rejecting the tradition of the past seeking to discover everything for himself would not get very far. It is also most unlikely that he would succeed in making any significant contribution to the tradition.

A third point of similarity lies in the relationship between the reality which a scientist experiences and his interpretation of it. The reality which he examines exists outside himself. It is something which he experiences in a variety of ways. His interpretation of it translates his experience into propositional forms which are ways of explaining its meaning and significance. What he must not do is to give ultimate authority to those propositional forms and, for example, treat an equation which describes the way certain materials behave or the way in which chemicals react as if it were a literal description of reality.

Present-day scientists who are aware of the dangers of using the word *literal* as if it meant the same as *real* recognize the need for a variety of models to explain the facts and do not suppose that what they are seeking to explain is not real if the models do not precisely correspond with human empirical experience. It is a great pity that some modern theologians do not appear to be aware of this danger and fail to realize that in common speech *literal* is taken to mean the same as *real*.

These similarities in themselves should make us realize the impossibility of the Church attempting to decide at a stroke whether a particular expression of the reality we experience is true or not. It just cannot be done, either by an individual or by a corporate body, even by a unanimous vote, still less by a majority vote in such a body. The truth of such an expression is tested by the extent to which it accords with the facts and the experience of the Church so that it becomes part of the Church's mind. It is significant that whenever in the Great Councils of the Church the attempt has been made to make a decision on a matter about which the Church has not yet come to a common mind, the matter has always had to be reopened. One example can be taken from the fourth century during the debates on the Arian heresy. Two Councils, that at Ariminum in the West and that at Seleucia in the East in 359 decided to adopt Arian formularies and it was in that year that Jerome wrote his famous words, 'The world woke up and groaned to find itself Arian.' But these decisions did not end the matter which had to be reconsidered by the Council of Constantinople in 381. A more recent example is to be seen in the Councils of Vatican I and Vatican II. Certain expressions and ways of thought to be found in the decrees of Vatican I never gained general acceptance and had to be reformulated in the decrees of Vatican II. It still remains to be seen to what extent the decrees of Vatican II will be endorsed not only by the Roman Catholic Church as a whole but by the whole Christian community.

How far then does what has been said apply to doctrinal expressions or decisions about doctrine within the Church? This question leads us to the first of the differences between the realm of the Church and that of the scientist. Although scientists do band themselves together in various voluntary associations such as the Royal Society or the British Association for the Advancement of Science, there is no universal society to which scientists belong and which is committed to the philosophy and methods which are the basis of scientific work. Nor is it even necessary to belong to one of those voluntary associations to be a scientist and work as one. The Church of God, by contrast, is a body which exists independently of its members and which as a body is committed to certain beliefs about its origin and purpose. Anyone can ask to be a member. The requirements are penitence and faith. It is not necessary to have certain educational qualifications, to be of a particular temperament, to have certain skills or to experience certain emotions.

Membership is voluntary in the sense that no one is compelled to belong but not in the sense that voluntary adherence on our part makes us members. We are made members by an act of God in his love and power through Baptism. The neophyte having declared his penitence and his faith in God is then asked, 'Do you desire Baptism?' as the means by which he is to be incorporated into the reality of the Body of Christ. However inadequate his understanding of the faith which he has professed, he then belongs to a Body which by its very nature is committed to certain dogmas. The word *dogma* is, of course, a word which has had a bad press but discussion about decision-making in the Church makes it imperative to use it. By way of introduction it is worth remembering what Dorothy L. Sayers wrote in 1940:

> Teachers and preachers never, I think, make it sufficiently clear that dogmas are not a set of arbitrary regulations invented *a priori* by a committee of theologians enjoying a burst of all-in dialectical wrestling. Most of them were hammered out under pressure of urgent practical necessity to provide an answer to heresies.[2]

The dogmas of the Church represent the considered and authoritative expression of the meaning of the facts upon which the Church depends and which it is committed to proclaim. They can be said to represent the formal acceptance of those facts, the reality of which is experienced in the life of the Church and which must be definitive for its life. The Church on earth, at any one time, is committed to these dogmas. Those who within its structure have the responsibility of teaching and preaching in its name and by its authority are required to make public profession of those dogmas. The Church as a whole is committed to living by them and to working out their implications for its life. The necessary task of theological thought and of seeking to express the gospel in a way which commends it to each generation has to be tested by those dogmas. The extent to which the Church succeeds in doing so will depend upon many factors and will vary from age to age. The

Church does not progress steadily from a past revelation to an eventual eternity, each successive generation being more successful in understanding it. The present is as T. S. Eliot said, 'The intersection of the timeless moment': the intersection of time and eternity just as each moment is a moment of judgement. It is a moment of eternity and a moment of judgement because each moment is a meeting with reality, the reality which is God himself and the reality of his creation.

In its life the Church has to make decisions about belief and decisions about actions, decisions which inevitably reflect the extent to which the Church is being obedient to the revelation given by God in Christ through the Spirit. Some of these decisions will be at an international level. An example of this in the Anglican Communion is the Lambeth Conference. Decisions also are made at a national level such as those in the General Synod of the Church of England. Others are made at a diocesan and a parochial level. In every case what matters is whether the decisions are made in the light of the fact that the Church lives under the judgement of revelation.

That revelation is made present and transmitted by the Church in a rich variety of ways. Through worship, preaching, the reading of the Scriptures, the administration of the Sacraments, the teaching of bishops and synods; through drawing upon the inheritance of the past in the teaching of the Fathers and the Masters of the spiritual life, through the work of theologians, the revelation of God in Christ is made alive and effective through the Spirit. But it is made alive and effective to a 'mixed' body of saints and sinners all of whom have to stand under its judgement and none of whom is capable of apprehending it fully in its richness and glory. Such a body needs a structure and a touchstone which ever remind it of that fact and which, at the same time, provide the freedom for the Church to develop and grow in its understanding and acquire the discernment to make decisions which reflect and embody revelation.

The dogmas of the Church are embodied in formularies such as the Creeds. By themselves they are not sufficient to express the meaning of the faith to each generation and the Church has the responsibility of expounding that meaning in an intelligible and persuasive way. The function of the formularies is to act as a touchstone.

They are given authority within the Church to provide a means by which the Church's thought and speculation can be tested. In one sense a certain parallel can be drawn between the testing of a scientific hypothesis and the testing of speculation within the Church. Just as any scientific hypothesis has to stand examination against empirical facts as they are observed so the theological thought within the Church has to be tested by the formularies in so far as they reflect and embody the revelation which is given in holy Scripture within the life of the Church itself. None of the decision-making bodies within the Church can say that a particular theological opinion is absolutely true. The most they can say and they have a right to say it, is that it does not contradict the statements which are made in the formularies and should therefore and can be examined by the Church to see if it becomes part of the Church's mind. If, however, such opinions contradict what is in the formularies then the Church must say that it is not acceptable and does not represent Christian tradition. Likewise, in the realms of order, that is the structure of the Church, which cannot be isolated from its beliefs, it has the responsibility of preventing any change in that order which would have the effect of committing the Church to the denial of a fundamental dogma or of preventing a legitimate interpretation of a fundamental dogma from being used by some of its members.

During its life the Church of God on earth has always been tempted to give authority to its institutions which is not justified. Professor Langmead Casserley was referring to this temptation when he spoke of the

> error of neglecting or ignoring the mystical character of the Church and, having first identified the Church with the Church militant, we then proceed either to identify the Church militant with its institutions or worse to define the Church militant in terms of its institutions.[3]

Elsewhere he writes:

> To survive with enduring identity, to maintain continuity through history, to change and yet remain the same thing, the Church, although not an institution, must yet possess and use social institutions, for its institutional continuities are both the means and embodiment of historical survival. Nevertheless the

103

essence of the Church must not be identified with its institutions nor can it be conceived and defined in terms of them.[4]

The Church of God on earth is not a democracy but a theocracy. To quote Professor Casserley again:

> In the Church man abdicates his arrogant claim to sovereignty and worships and adores the absolute sovereignty of God. We may well say that it is only this theocratic attitude towards life which sanctions and upholds the values of earthly democracy at any sufficiently deep philosophical level but we must add that nevertheless the Church in the last analysis is theocratic and not democratic.[5]

At the same time, because living the revelation is a function to be performed by the whole Church of God, it is right and proper that every member of the Church should have a part to play as it seeks to live by the revelation which brought it into existence. But that is not to say that an institution which provides for such participation is or can be infallible. The Church of England in its Articles of Religion accepts the fact that Councils being composed of fallible men can err. No institution within the Church, be it the papacy or a parochial church council, should arrogate to itself an authority which lies in revelation alone and apply it to statements or definitions about the faith which it makes.

The reasons for this are twofold. First, it is because any human institution is composed of fallible men. The second reason follows from the previous discussion about the nature of truth and springs from the way in which human beings have to respond to reality. Corporate bodies, however representative, cannot decide whether certain statements are absolutely true. The most they can do is to decide whether or not they accord with the facts in the case of science or with dogmas to which the Church is committed in the case of the Church. As I have pointed out on earlier occasions, it would have been laughable if, when Einstein had produced his theory of relativity, the scientists of the world had supposed that by convening a thoroughly representative body of scientists, a decision could have been taken by a vote as to whether or not the theory was true. Einstein himself regarded his theory as defective though preferable to Newton's theory and spent the remainder of his life trying to improve it. Had such a conference of scientists been convened the most that could have happened would be for some empirical evidence to have been produced which was inimical to the theory.

In its approach to theological truth, the Church of England has traditionally reflected the distinction between the revelation to which the Church owes its origin and existence, the fundamental dogmas of which are expressed in the title deeds of the Church of England, and the expression of that revelation by a particular generation to its time. Such a distinction is, for example, reflected in the 1938 report 'Doctrine in the Church of England'. What is new in the present situation is first that the title deeds are being questioned, and secondly that as will be seen, their authority is undermined by the power given to the General Synod, a situation which is reflected in the kind of decisions asked from diocesan and deanery synods.

Comprehensiveness has traditionally been regarded as a distinctive characteristic of the Church of England and of the Anglican Communion. The word is, however, used to described what are essentially two different qualities. It is sometimes used in a way which reflects the fact that the Church of England claims to be both Catholic and Reformed and manifests in its life elements which are in continuity with Catholic tradition and elements which have been absorbed from the Reformation. It is also used to describe the way by which the Church lives and expresses its theology. The Church of England appeals neither to an infallible pope nor to the authority of one particular theologian such as Luther or Calvin as being definitive, but trusts that by the guidance of the Holy Spirit the truth of revelation will become evident in the life of the Church as it worships, prays, thinks and debates.

Comprehensiveness in the first sense expressed itself in precise forms. On the Catholic side the traditional threefold form of the Apostolic ministry was retained; the ancient Creeds were embodied in liturgical rites and defined as authoritative; the dominical Sacraments were retained as 'generally necessary to Salvation'; the pattern of worship was essentially Catholic, with the Eucharist at the centre (at least in intention if not always in subsequent practice) flanked by the Morning and Evening Prayer drawn very skilfully from the former offices of the Breviary; finally the decrees of the first four General Councils were defined as authoritative.

On the Reformed side, holy Scripture was proclaimed to be the touchstone of tradition and the Articles of Religion made clear where the Church of England stood on the burning controversies of the sixteenth century. As Bishop Stephen Neill has put it:

> Their purpose is to make clear the position of a Church which sets before it the aim of being Catholic, avoiding on the one hand the late mediaeval traditions of Rome and on the other the excesses of the Anabaptists.[6]

There is no doubt that the Church of England took great pains to preserve the great central truths of the Christian religion. This is clear from an examination of its formularies. But it also made possible differing opinions on many subordinate matters, some of them of great importance. It distinguishes between those doctrines which are necessary for salvation and other permissible doctrines and makes holy Scripture the touchstone for determining the former. Every bishop or priest is committed to the distinction at the time of his consecration or ordination, explicitly if the Prayer Book rite is used and implicitly if that in the Alternative Service Book. The classical theologians in the Church of England have pointed out that it has traditionally only regarded a particular belief as heretical if it is contrary to those truths which were made conditions of communion by formal decrees of the undivided Universal Church, and that side by side with an insistence on such fundamental truths it has allowed more opinions than one in regard to many matters about which no such action was taken by the Church as a whole. This position reflected the provisions of the Act of Supremacy, 1559 which were reaffirmed by the Lambeth Conference, 1867 which stated:

> We Bishops of Christ's Holy Catholic Church, professing the faith of the primitive and undivided Church, as based on Scripture, defined by the first four General Councils (see 1. Eliz. C.1 36) and reaffirmed by the Fathers of the English Reformation.

It follows that for a purely Anglican body to require a particular interpretation, in a matter which has not been ecumenically decided and to attempt to unchurch those who cannot accept it, is contrary to the doctrinal basis of the Church of England.

Comprehensiveness in this sense provided a clear framework of

Scripture, Creed, Sacrament and Ministry, together with a Prayer Book by which doctrine was to be expressed in worship. This framework enabled comprehensiveness in the other sense to be expressed. Professor H. E. W. Turner has described this kind of comprehensiveness as a dialectic faith, a faith that deliberately accepts the tension between different points of view. Such an understanding of comprehensiveness represents a belief that given an accepted framework and agreement on fundamentals of the Christian faith, there should be a measure of freedom in interpretation. It represents a belief that the Church should eschew heresy trials and new definitions of doctrine. It should be prepared to accept the strains and tensions of controversy and debate within itself in the belief that through such debate the Church will come to a deeper understanding of the truth. Such a way of learning to live the truth puts great demands upon the members of the Church, but Anglicans believe it to be the right way. It is perhaps the fact that it makes heavy demands which has led to comprehensiveness being regarded not as the expression of a dialectic faith but of a compromise of moderation. We need to grasp the opportunity provided by the Anglican situation for

> positive and creative discussion and fellowship between groups with the one aim of discovering by the guidance of the Holy Spirit what in each tradition witnesses to an essential element of scriptural and catholic truth, what in each tradition is lacking, and in what way each tradition, because it has to some degree developed in isolation, has become distorted.[7]

If such creative discussion is to take place the tension must be both contained and maintained. It must be contained because completely open-ended discussion is seldom fruitful. Dialectic requires tension or compression and they can only exist within limits. To accept a degree of freedom of interpretation requires that there should be some accepted expression of what is regarded as essential for the life of the Church.

The framework described above under the first meaning of comprehensiveness provides that expression. Appeal to it has been made in moments of stress in the life of the Anglican Communion, which has thereby been enabled to survive.

Two developments have taken place in recent years which have threatened the life of the Anglican Communion as never before; so much so that even one as passionately committed to the Anglican expression of the Christian faith as Bishop Stephen Neill can write, 'The first and burning question is naturally whether the Anglican Communion in anything like its present form can survive at all.'[8]

The first development which has led to this is the dismantling of the framework. The Book of Common Prayer is no longer one of the chief bonds which unites Anglicans all over the world. Further, the great diversity in liturgical rites throughout the world makes it impossible to appeal to them as a doctrinal standard as was possible with the Book of Common Prayer. Because of the principle *lex orandi, lex credendi,*—the law of worship is the law of faith—which has always been held in Anglicanism it is no longer possible to appeal to a common doctrine expressed in the Church's worship. Not only are the Creeds as expressions of doctrine under fire; so are the doctrines they express. The Thirty-Nine Articles have largely been abandoned in the Anglican Communion, though in some Provinces they are retained as a purely historical document. The authority of holy Scripture has been seriously undermined to such an extent that it has been argued that 'appropriateness' and 'expediency' are the only criteria for determining the rightness of theological decisions and action.

The ordination of women in the provinces of the Anglican Communion has jeopardized the claim of Anglicans to be within the Catholic tradition. It destroys the claim made in the 1920 Lambeth Appeal that we have a ministry which could be 'acknowledged by every part of the Church as possessing not only the inward call of the Spirit but also the commission of Christ and the authority of the whole body.'

The dismantling of the framework raises enough questions for the Anglican Communion. It has already brought disunity and distress. But it has been accompanied by a fundamental change in the way in which authority is given to doctrinal statements. The traditional Anglican approach was expressed in the Report 'Doctrine in the Church of England' published in 1938:

> The Church's understanding of the Gospel is continually renewed by its experience of communion with God through Christ; and the authority of its doctrinal formulations ought always to be accepted as resting, at least in part, upon the acceptance of these by the whole body of the faithful. This

authority, in so far as it is devised from such a *consensus fidelium*, rests upon the range and quality of the manifold experience which that *consensus* gathers up, and upon the witness, which alike in the devotional and other practice of Christians generally and in the doctrine of the theologians, it bears to the truth of the Gospel. The weight of the *consensus fidelium* does not depend upon mere numbers or on the extension of a belief at any one time, but on continuance through the ages and the extent to which the *consensus* is genuinely free.[9]

The exercise of such an approach demands time and patience, whereas in recent years there has emerged what can be described as instant theology. It is the practice of purporting to determine the truth in matters of doctrine, morals or of liturgical and sacramental practice with doctrinal implications by a majority vote in a provincial or diocesan body after an hour or two's debate, or by the uncritical acceptance of the report of a working party or commission in the composition of which the Church as a whole has little say. Some matters can rightly be so decided and the decision loyally accepted. Decisions purporting to determine truth cannot so be made and not only in the realm of doctrine. Yet this is what is happening, as can be illustrated by three examples. The resolution passed by the Lambeth Conference in 1968 about the Service of Reconciliation in the Anglican-Methodist Scheme when it was admitted that many bishops had not had an opportunity to read the Scheme was widely regarded as a declaration of its theological rightness.

The Anglican Consultative Council established by the Lambeth Conference in 1968 has, notwithstanding its terms of reference which stress its consultative nature, not hesitated to make decisions which, in effect, determine theological matters of universal significance, as in its resolution on Polygamy (Resolution 25 of ACC 2) or in its resolution asking provinces to declare that deaconesses be declared to be within the Diaconate (Resolution 11 of ACC 3). It is somewhat ironical that when the essentially consultative and advisory nature of the Lambeth Conference is again being stressed, the ACC is not reluctant to give directions to the Provinces of the Anglican Communion on controversial matters. The third example is the debate on the ordination of women in the General Synod of the Church of England in July 1975, when notwithstanding the fact that many Christians in the Roman Catholic and Orthodox Churches, as well as a substantial minority of the General Synod itself (which turned out to be 41%) held different opinions, it resolved that there were no fundamental objections, some of those voting for the Resolution subsequently arguing that this determined the truth in the matter.

Instant theology produces grave difficulties in the purely doctrinal sphere when such decisions conflict with existing formularies. But at least they remain as a court of appeal. It has much more serious results which it is used to justify and authorize action in the realms of order or liturgy based upon the theological judgement made. What was a theological opinion becomes part of the *lex orandi*. It is deeply divisive in that when such a decision is based on a majority vote it ignores the position of the minority and places an intolerable strain upon their consciences. It is extraordinary that at a time when in the world generally so much is spoken about liberty from oppression, consciences should be so oppressed in this way.

Much more important is the fact that instant theology represents a fundamental change in the Anglican approach to truth and to theological debate. As the Dean of St Albans writes:

> It is true that we live in an age of instant decision, instant food, instant demands. The Church must beware of so identifying itself with the contemporary scene that it falls victim to a similar state of mind.[10]

The Church of England has traditionally made its commitment to revelation clear in its title deeds. They themselves reflect the fact that they are but the expression of a divine revelation supremely expressed in holy Scripture and in the historical events of our redemption and recognize the fact that they are subject to its authority. On the other hand, it has allowed freedom within the limits set by those title deeds for truth to express itself and emerge from the life of the community. Censorship, examination for orthodoxy and control of teaching are alien to its ethos. Such things as trials for heresy are very rare and when they have occurred have taken place in courts which are based on the secular criteria of interpretation rather than on those of an ecclesiastical forum. Some may feel that the Church of England has erred on the side of too much liberty and too little attention has been paid in the past to its title deeds. Others will rejoice that in the past it has not sought to give authority to any particular body as definitive of the Faith and has accepted the ultimate authority of revelation and of Scripture.

In recent years however, a very significant change has taken place, so much so that some members of the General Synod have been heard to express the desire for those who cannot accept a particular change to leave the Church of England. While the title deeds of the Church of England remain as in the past, the doctrinal authority has been placed in the hands of the General Synod. As has been said, the extent to which this has happened is not always realized and the Church Assembly in passing the necessary legislation (and Parliament in approving it) seems to have forgotten Article XXI which recognizes that a General Council, and by implication a National Council, may err.

The Church of England (Worship and Doctrine) Measure 1974 gave the General Synod the power to determine whether any statement of belief or action was in fact in accordance with the Doctrine of the Church of England. That Measure enabled the General Synod to make provision by Canon with respect to worship in the Church of England and other matters presented by the Book of Common Prayer and with respect to the obligation and forms of assent or subscription to the Doctrine of the Church of England. The Measure provides *inter alia* that (1) the Forms of Services contained in the Book of Common Prayer continue to be available for use in the Church of England (2) any Canon passed under the Measure shall have effect notwithstanding anything inconsistent therein contained in any of the rubrics of the Book of Common Prayer (3) it shall be lawful for the Synod to make provision by Canon with respect to the obligations of the clergy, deaconesses and lay officers to assent or subscribe to the Doctrine of the Church of England.

The change to which I have just referred however, is effected by the clause in the Measure which provides that in the opinion of the General Synod no Canon which is passed under the Measure is either contrary to or indicative of any departure from the Doctrine of the Church of England. It also provides that the final approval by the General Synod of any such Canon or Regulation or form of Service or amendment thereof shall conclusively determine that the Synod is of such opinion as aforesaid in respect of the matter so approved.

Graham Leonard

It is commonly supposed that the formularies of the Church of England provide a doctrinal standard by which the various institutions of government in the Church of England have to act. At first sight in the light of the provision that the General Synod may not make any provision which is contrary to or indicative of any departure from the Doctrine of the Church of England in any essential matter it might seem that such is the case. Consideration of the powers of the General Synod however, would seem to indicate that this is not so, for it lies within the power of Synod to determine whether or not any provision indicates any such departure and the mere fact of approval being given 'conclusively determines' the matter. In other words, a majority vote whether special or not, determines a matter of truth rather than the interpretation of a formulary or doctrinal standard. Action is then taken upon the decison, and freedom of interpretation is thereby denied.

During the debates in the General Synod on the Worship and Doctrine Measure objections were repeatedly raised at every stage to the giving of such power to the General Synod. By way of reply the question was always asked, 'What body shall have doctrinal authority in the Church of England if it is not to be the General Synod'. This question assumes, however, that a representative body can possess the power to make doctrinal decisions. This would appear to represent falling into the temptation to try and give authority to an institution within the Church which it cannot and should not possess and to reflect a wrong understanding of how the Church seeks to live by the truth to which it is committed.

In other words, the General Synod has been made judge of the title deeds rather than allowing the title deeds to express the revelation which they seek to embody and by which it must be judged.

The legal position, whether statutory or canonical, appears to be confused. *Halsbury's Ecclesiastical Law* states that :

Synodical Government is not to be interpreted as meaning that all the functions of church government are concentrated in or subject to the control of the General Synod; account must be taken not only of the royal supremacy, and of the ultimate legislative authority of Parliament, but also of the authority and powers exercised independently of the General Synod by the bishops, the ecclesiastical courts and the Church Commissioners.[11]

But when discussing the doctrinal standards which are capable of being enforced by the Courts, Halsbury refers to the Revised Canons and in particular to Canon A5 'Of the Doctrine of the Church of England' which reads as follows:

> The doctrine of the Church of England is grounded in the Holy Scriptures, and in such teachings of the ancient Fathers and Councils of the Church as are agreeable to the said Scriptures. In particular such doctrine is to be found in the Thirty-Nine Articles of Religion, the Book of Common Prayer and the Ordinal.

Yet under the Worship and Doctrine Measure the interpretation of this Canon is, in effect, in the hands of the General Synod.

It is difficult to have any confidence in the way in which the General Synod exercises its power of interpretation, and as the Bishop of Chichester has made clear in his Chapter attempts have been made to undermine such safeguards as exist, inadequate though they are, to control the Synod in its doctrinal judgements.

The term *consensus fidelium* is of vital importance in deciding doctrinal matters. It must not be interpreted as if it were simply referring to decisions of synodical bodies, as if a majority vote actually determined the truth and expressed the mind of the Church. In the November 1984 group of sessions of General Synod, the Archbishop of Canterbury spoke about the need for a common mind:

> There are six matters on the agenda—five motions and one amendment—which affect in one way or another the order of the Church of England, holy orders in the Church of England. I would just like to put down one or two points which we need to keep in mind.
>
> We hear much use of the magic word 'consensus'. Nobody seems to know what it means; everyone seems to have his or her own interpretation of it. This Synod is not here to find a consensus but to find a common mind. This is important. This Synod has been given, through the Enabling Act, through the Synodical Government Measure, freedom to make and change

its doctrine. If it has that, it needs to take very seriously the method by which it does so. We have already heard this morning some of our dislike of a long stop. But if we have not got a long stop we need to look very carefully at the way in which we do our business before we start thinking about changing the rules. Then we need to look at history. Sometimes it is so easy to think of the cult of the passing moment, and we forget where our roots are. We believe ourselves to be the Catholic Church in this country. Our roots must be in history, in the apostolic Church, in the general councils and in the Church throughout the ages. We need to look at the Church catholic. I was ordained a priest of the Church of God, not the Church of England, and our holy orders are that which we share with the whole Church. Therefore, we need to look at the whole Church when we are considering this. I say these things merely to put down a marker.[12]

It is a great pity that the General Synod did not take heed of the Archbishop's words in the subsequent debate on the ordination of women.

How then should the Church of England make decisions on issues involving doctrine which, on its own professed basis, include those concerned with church order?

First, it must accept the implications of its own claim to be Catholic as well as Reformed and must refrain from trying to act as if it were autonomous.

Secondly, it must accept that the aim of any definition must be as limited as possible and confined to fundamental doctrines, leave as much open as possible to different interpretations provided that such interpretations do not deny those fundamentals and provided that action in the realm of order does not impugn them nor prejudge their interpretation.

Thirdly, it must recognize that only thus will it exercise its responsibility for maintaining the unity of the Church. To attempt to define doctrine unnecessarily or to promote action which prejudges doctrinal agreement can only result either in the stifling of consciences or division or possibly both. This should never be right or necessary when what is at stake is an issue on which there is either no common mind in the Church, or where there can be a legitimate diversity of interpretation.

Fourthly, it must accept that the onus for justifying change lies with those who promote it. The Articles of Religion make it quite clear that 'although the Church be a witness and keeper of Holy Writ, yet, as it ought not to decree any thing against the same, so besides the same ought it not to enforce any thing to be believed for the necessity of Salvation[13] and in the Prayer Book Ordinal, still a source of the doctrine of the Church of England, prayer is made for the newly ordained priests that they may deliver what is in the holy Word of God or what is agreeable to the same. In other words, it is not just a question of *Nihil obstat*—is there any reason why not? What is proposed must be shown to be agreeable to Scripture. To enforce action which gives expression to interpretation where there is not agreement, can put people in the situation where they are required to accept as necessary what cannot be required as necessary for eternal salvation.

There are clearly many issues on which the General Synod can properly decide though great care must be taken to limit these to those which do not have a fundamental doctrinal import.

If the General Synod is to act responsibly and to win respect and authority, three things are necessary.

First, it must reaffirm the doctrinal basis of the Church of England and its unequivocal acceptance of Canon A5.

Secondly, it must accept that such authority as it possesses is a derived authority and that it exercises such authority under the judgement of what is revealed in holy Scripture.

Thirdly, it must accept that in the realm of fundamental doctrines, or of action which relates to them, its duty is not to make decisions, even by special majority, but to take all possible steps for such matters to be considered within the Church of England, the Anglican Communion and ecumenically so that a common mind can emerge. While that process continues, it should not prejudge any issue by actions.

It may seem as if such conditions will preclude discussion and development. On the contrary, they make it possible without impugning the very *raison d'être* of the Church. Without them, the Church of England will cease to be part of the Catholic Church and will degenerate into a club composed of those who hold a variety of opinions. What is true biologically of a living organism is true of the Body of Christ on earth. If its structure is preserved, a living organism shows astonishing powers of adaptation in accordance

115

with its essential nature. Destroy the structure and not only is the power of adaptation lost but it ceases to be itself.

NOTES

1 Rom. 12.1-2 NEB (alternative translation).
2 Sayers, D. L., *Creed or Chaos* (London 1949), p. 34.
3 Casserley, J. Langmead, *Christian Community* (1960), p. 23.
4 ibid., p. 32.
5 ibid., p. 33.
6 Neill, S. C., *Anglicanism*, revised edn (Oxford 1977), p. 81.
7 Buchanan, C. O., Leonard, G. D., Mascall, E. L., Packer, J. I., *Growing into Union* (Nottingham 1970), p.23.
8 Neill, op. cit., p. 388.
9 *Doctrine in the Church of England* (London 1928), p. 35.
10 Moore, Peter, ed., *Man, Woman and Priesthood* (London 1978).
11 *Halsbury's Ecclesiastical Law*, 4th edn (1975), para 385, n.1.
12 *Report of Proceedings* 15/3, p. 860.
13 *Articles of Religion* XX.

8

The Church of England and Parliament

Enoch Powell

All questions which concern the Church of England, as do questions on the General Synod and its relations with Parliament, presuppose an answer to the question: what is the Church of England? That is to say, what is its essential characteristic, without which it would be something different in kind? I must, therefore, before I write about the General Synod and Parliament, make clear my own answer to that question. The Church of England is that Church of which the Supreme Governor on earth is the Crown of England. This description applies to no other Church, or part of the Church, and it applies to the Church of England irrespective of all other characteristics and of doctrine. Its essential nature is thus not doctrinal but political.

The Church of England may be in communion with other Churches, implying mutual recognition of the validity of each other's orders and sacraments. This does not make those other Churches part of the Church of England. The doctrines and liturgy of the Church of England are shared by other Churches throughout the world which were planted by it or derived from it; but the Anglican Communion, as the totality of those Churches is called, is not the Church of England, although the latter and its members are often described and often describe themselves as *Anglican*.

This relationship of the Anglican Communion with the Church of England is at least potentially at odds with the latter's essential characteristic. The Anglican Communion, being episcopal, has always voluntarily recognized the Primate of all England as its president or chief prelate; and Archbishops of Canterbury, including the present one, have tended to pay great regard to, and derive much satisfaction from, this world-wide position, travelling about the continents like Paul VI and John Paul II, almost as if they were popes themselves.

Not one of the other Churches in the Anglican Communion is governed by the supreme lay or secular authority in its own territory. They are self-governing or synodical churches, as have become, for instance, the Church in Wales and the Church of Ireland, since the English Crown renounced the supreme government of the church in those territories. The Archbishop and the General Synod of the Church of England are thus unique among the prelates and synods of the Anglican Communion, in that they are, by the essential nature of the Church of England, respectively appointed by the Crown and subordinate to the governorship of the Crown. Membership, not to say leadership, of the Anglican Communion is thus apt to predispose the prelates and the General Synod to be impatient and intolerant of that very royal supremacy which is essential to the definition of the Church of England. If all other Anglican prelates are elected, they think, why not they? If all other Anglican synods are sovereign in doctrine and in church government, why not the General Synod?

The Crown of England which became Supreme Governor of the Church of England in the sixteenth century had not yet placed almost its whole prerogative in commission with Parliament. This constitutional development has had the consequence that the Crown which is Supreme Governor of the church is a crown that acts on the advice of Ministers and legislates with the advice and consent of Parliament. It is a parliamentary crown, and the Church of England is accordingly a parliamentary church, not because Parliament represents the Church of England or is representative of the members of the Church of England, but because the supreme authority in this realm is the Crown in Parliament.

What is unique about the Church of England is not so much that its Supreme Governor is royal as that its supreme authority is lay or secular. In that respect the Church of England resembles the fourth-century conciliar church, whose catholicity—we English call it *uniformity*—was guaranteed by its subordination to the Imperial authority. It is a characteristic which the western church lost with the fall of the Roman Empire but which England regained by the assertion of complete sovereign independence in its own territory.

For the Church of England is territorial. It is of necessity the Church *in* England which the Crown governs. That preposition *in* is significant and fruitful. *Ecclesia anglicana* before the Reformation meant the Church in England, that is, the part of the Church which subsisted in England. It was over that Church in England that the Crown became Supreme Governor. Logically its governorship extended no farther than the outer limits of its territorial sovereignty. Equally logically it applied to everybody within that territory, whence, despite the rise and toleration of other churches and of irreligion, the Church of England is still the Church of every resident in every parish throughout England: he may not claim it, but if he does his claim is upheld by the law. It is the Church of all the English, of all in England, precisely because, and only because, the supreme authority in it is the supreme secular authority. No other Church in the Anglican Communion can occupy the same position in its own country.

Of course the counterpart of the inclusiveness of the Church of Englnd is its geographical exclusiveness: only an Englishman— strictly speaking, only an inhabitant of England—can be Church of England—others may be Anglicans, if they see fit.

The automatic and permanent consequence of the royal supremacy was, and is, that the legislature of the Church of England is no other than Parliament. Whatever legislative power the Convocations of Canterbury and York possessed in the Middle Ages, they surrendered it in May 1532, and the surrender was confirmed in 1534 by the Act for the Submission of the Clergy. The royal supremacy over the Church in England was established by the Crown in Parliament. The instrument that Henry VIII used for doing so was the omnicompetence of Parliament, and thenceforward the law ecclesiastical no less than the law temporal would be made in England by Parliament. The foundation deeds of the Church in England, the *Ecclesia anglicana,* by custom translated *Church of England,* are Acts of the so-called Reformation Parliament 1529–36. Repealed under Philip and Mary, they were reinstated by the Act of Supremacy of 1559. The Book of Common Prayer and the Articles were given legal force by statutes of 1559 and 1571 respectively.

After making the canons of 1604, which, not having been enacted by Parliament, did not have the force of law, the Convocations atrophied and eventually, between 1717 and 1850, were nonexistent altogether. They were revived in the second half of last century as forums of clerical debate, but they could of course have no legislative function.

By the time of the First World War, however, the assumption became prevalent that a body of law basically almost four centuries old was going to require amendment and extension. Meanwhile Parliament and Government had ceased, by virtue of religious toleration, to be identifiable with the Church of England, so that neither the preparation or initiation of legislation appeared to be appropriate functions for government nor the detailed debate and scrutiny of legislative proposals appropriate functions for the two Houses of Parliament. Those functions would have to be performed, therefore, it was argued, by some other body or bodies which *were* identifiable with the Church.

The solution of the problem adopted in 1919 was to create a new body by adding to the upper (episcopal) and lower (clerical) houses of Convocation a third element which should be lay and elective, and to enable measures duly sent forward to Parliament from that body to be given the force of law by the Crown in Parliament through a summary procedure. Profound and difficult issues of principle were raised or rather, implicitly, burked by the Church of England (Powers) Act 1919, which embodied that solution.

Devolution of legislative authority by the Houses of Parliament subject to a simple affirmative or negative vote has always been a ticklish matter. It is true that statutes have conferred upon Ministers of the Crown powers to make subordinate legislation, where the regulations or orders are themselves unamendable and are affirmed or negatived as they stand by the two Houses. These powers however are exercised by those responsible to Parliament, which can and sometimes does compel them either to withdraw and alter the proposed legislation or to drop it altogether.

If anyone should object that on joining the Economic European Community in 1972 Parliament did in fact pass to an external body, for the first time in at least four centuries, the right to legislate over its head, I would caution him against deducing from this *gran rifiuto* that Parliament will easily submit to a similar renunciation in any other direction. It remains a fearsome thing, from which powerful Ministers, like monarchs before them, have shrunk, to say to the House of Commons: 'This you must pass, and pass unaltered.'

One disagreeable consequence of legislation put forward to Parliament for its approval by another body is that Parliament is thereby deprived of the opportunity to exert its most fruitful legislative activity on behalf of the subject, namely, to question and examine in detail each and every separate provision and formulation.

These fundamental drawbacks of delegated legislation are enhanced rather than lessened by the procedure used in relation to measures which the General Synod passes and submits to Parliament for approval. They are, before submission to either House, considered by a statutory joint select committee of both Houses, which is empowered to take evidence, including evidence offered on behalf of the General Synod, and is known as the Ecclesiastical Committee. The Committee lays before each House a report of any evidence taken and its opinion whether or not the measure is 'expedient'.

In the House of Commons measures of the General Synod are proposed for approval by the Second Church Commissioner, a Member who is a Government appointee but not a member of the Government, and no responsibility for them is formally taken by the Government. Nevertheless it is the almost invariable custom for a government to support such measures by putting through the division lobbies, if necessary, what is known as the 'payroll vote', that is, Ministers and such hangers-on as have their bread buttered on the Government side. The consequence is that in effect the Government passes General Synod measures without taking responsibility for them.[1] True, the Ecclesiastical Committee will have reported to both Houses as to a Measure's 'expediency, especially in its relation to the constitutional rights of all Her Majesty's subjects'; but despite the generality of the term 'expediency' and the vagueness of 'constitutional rights', it has interpreted its terms of reference narrowly, on the basis of a philosophy which excludes considerations of policy and principle on such grounds as are discussed in this Chapter and might be brought forward in debate in either House. Very rarely does the Committee induce the Synod, through the latter's Legislative Committee, to withdraw a proposed Measure with a view to submitting it again in a modified form.

There is thus an ultimate incompatibility between the legislative supremacy of Parliament and the legislative functions of the General Synod under the Church of England Assembly Act, 1919. This always existed potentially from the start. It would become practical and intractable if there were, for instance, on the part of the General Synod a presumption that Parliament is bound to approve Measures of the Synod if declared 'expedient' by the Ecclesiastical Committee—which is tantamount to telling the House of Commons to function as a rubber stamp. For any body to accept the obligation so to function is to acknowledge that it is not sovereign. The presumption would therefore be in itself a repudiation of the royal supremacy and thus of the essential nature of the Church of England.

There are two distinct grounds on which that presumption could be argued. One is that the General Synod, inasmuch as it is duly representative of the Church of England, is alone entitled to take decisions about its government, worship and doctrine, irrespective of whether they require to be given effect by changing the law of England. The second ground is that Parliament is not of itself a fit authority to legislate for the Church of England. I will examine both these contentions on their own terms, although each is incompatible inherently with the continued existence of what I believe the Church of England to be.

The legislative authority of the Crown in Parliament has always been bound up with the idea of representation, i.e. with assent validly given on behalf of a larger body, such as the electorate, through a smaller body of persons duly elected for the purpose in a particular way defined by custom and precedent, and not otherwise. Hence the enactment of all legislation 'by and with the advice and consent of ... the Commons in this present Parliament assembled'. There is no other representation than this by the advice and consent of which the law can be made or changed on any subject. The local by-laws proposed by elected councils have to be enacted by Parliament; trades union law is not made by representatives (elected or not) of trades unionists, nor is commercial law by representatives (elected or not) of merchants or manufacturers. In short, election carries of itself no implication of legislative capacity: law purporting to be made by any wholly or partly elected body other than Parliament would be as horrid a tyranny as law made by individual caprice.

The Church Assembly acquired no claim to legislative competence by the fact that two of its three components comprised persons appointed to that component by a process of election, even though the elective representation of the clergy was different in kind in an important respect from the elective representation of the laity by the third component. The clergy, cathedral and diocesan, are a precisely definable and identifiable body of persons, and directly or indirectly all those persons take, or are entitled to take, part in the electoral process, a process, incidentally, which has been accepted as valid by those concerned over an extremely long, though not unbroken, period of time.

In the case of the laity, it is not only the electoral process itself—a process of cumulative indirect election through a hierarchy of electoral colleges—which has not been hallowed by habit and custom. The underlying electorate itself is open to question.

The electoral process is as follows. The annual parish meetings elect triennially the representatives of the respective parishes to form the House of Laity of the deanery synods. These Houses in turn elect the House of Laity of the diocesan synods. It is the Houses of Laity of the deanery synods which, when a General Synod is to be elected, choose the representatives who shall go from each diocese to the House of Laity of the General Synod.

There are three counts at least on which any claim to representative authority on the part of the House of Laity of the General Synod is open to question. First, there is the feature of indirect, collegiate election itself. The members of the House of Laity might, in some subtle sense, be held responsible to their diocesan synods for the action they take and the votes which they cast. What is certain is that they cannot be responsible through the diocesan and deanery synods to the underlying electorate, the membership of the annual parish meetings, who have been electing persons to sit in a deanery synod to deal with matters within the scope of that synod and not to take on their behalf the sort of decisions which the General Synod takes.

This flaw is closely linked with another, namely, that the parish elections which—albeit indirectly through the deanery synods—create the diocesan synods are not taking place with the General Synod in view or at a time when a new General Synod is to be elected. There is, so to speak, no such thing as a General Synod general election. Yet a general election is of the essence of the representative claim of the body elected. The underlying electorate at large is not able to mandate its representatives on the issues with which the new General Synod is expected to deal.

Individual members of the parish meeting are in no position to bind a candidate to vote, in circumstances which do not as yet exist, for a deanery candidate for the diocesan synod which will send representatives to the General Synod, so that these latter will vote one way rather than another on questions which are not before the electors who attend the annual meeting.

The most fundamental defect however lies in the nature of the underlying electorate itself: the persons on the parish electoral rolls. I will not make much of the attendance at parish meetings, nor inquire what percentage turn-out they represent of those whose names are on the rolls, though I suspect that the percentage would by any political standards be derisory. I ask rather: who are these people who are on the electoral rolls? They are qualified by habitual attendance at public worship during the previous six months. I concede that parish priests generally make an effort to ensure that as many as possible of such persons as are known to him do get onto the roll. But are those persons, in the necessary sense, the people—the *laos*—of the Church of England? The contrary would indeed follow automatically from my earlier proposition that the Church of England is the right and possession of all the people of England, both those who do and those who do not avail themselves of it, so that all the people of England are, as such, potentially members of the Church of England in a sense in which they can not be potentially members of the Roman or any other Church. But that is not what I am arguing here. I am here making the more limited claim that those whose worship and attendance are occasional, who are not even annually communicant, but who look to the Church of England to hallow the great events of their lives, are also entitled to be regarded as its laity and to be included in its representation. If so, the electorate which underlies the indirect, pyramidal election of the House of Laity of the General Synod is too narrow and partial to sustain a claim by that body to represent the Church of England for the purpose of consenting to changes in its law.

We have at this point come close to the nature of the other ground for the General Synod's claim to legislate for the Church of England, namely, that Parliament, and in particular the House of Commons, is not a fit authority to speak, or therefore to legislate, for the Church of England.

Let it first be reiterated that Parliament legislated, and legislates still, for the Church of England not as being representative of it but because the Crown, the Church's Supreme Governor, makes all law through Parliament and only through Parliament. It is as a representation of the whole realm that Parliament advises and consents on legislation. In so doing, it makes law for many parts or elements or interests in the nation of which it would not claim to be representative. It is doing that all the time, though most instructive is the fact that the law in Scotland and Wales and (albeit by a different procedure) Northern Ireland is made, where different from that of England, by the whole Parliament and the whole House of Commons—not, for instance, just by the Scottish peers and the M.P.s from Scotland alone. It is as much a function of the whole Parliament to legislate for the Church of England as to legislate for Wales.

Of course that is not the whole story. The House of Commons, believe it or not, is a highly reasonable body and proceeds in a commonsensical way to respect the views and wishes of those of its Members which it regards as particularly concerned or particularly knowledgeable. English constituency members do not generally orate upon Scottish affairs, taking it that the Scottish members are most involved in them and probably know more about them. If, indeed, an issue of general policy or of party division arises, the Government and its opponents will use their whips and there will be a full turn-out, if not in the Chamber, at any rate in the division lobbies. For the rest, however, Parliament, being a very English institution, tends to lean towards the English principle of 'live-and let-live'.

The House of Commons has not since the eighteenth century been exclusively Church of England. Religious surveys of its membership are not popular, but a recent estimate of a recent House of Commons produced a breakdown[2] in which the largest single denomination was, nominally at least, Church of England. Moreover, England, to which since Irish and Welsh disestablishment the Church of England has been territorially confined, returns out of the total of 650 members 523 who might be said to have a specifically constituency connection with the Church of England. The House of Commons is on these facts still a body in which many members would regard the Church of England's business as of concern to them, personally or as constituency representatives. Nor should it be supposed that Dissenters, Roman Catholics, Jews and those avowedly without personal religion are necessarily without interest in, or concern for, the Church of which the Sovereign is the Supreme Governor. Their contributions to debates on Church of England measures have sometimes been notable. There is thus nothing in the character or composition of Parliament or the House of Commons which makes grotesque in practice its constitutionally logical function as the legislator for the Church.

If, of course, it were to be demanded of Parliament that it should renounce that function—a renunciation, be it noted, which could only be simultaneous with the Crown's renunciation of the supreme government of the Church of England and consequently (on the definition here adopted) with the ending of the Church of England itself—Parliament would not resist. Admittedly Parliament in renouncing or transferring power is apt to be embarrassingly inquisitive about the status and bona fides of the recipient; and it is not at all certain that it would regard the General Synod as sufficiently in the image of Parliament to be entrusted with the powers which Parliament was renouncing.

However, it is necessary to be clear about what is the meaning of the word *demand* in this context. It means a demand from those whom Parliament represents which it cannot prudently refuse. Demands in that sense have been made and conceded before now—to Roman Catholics for enfranchisement and to Dissenters for civil recognition. It is the sort of demand for the detection of which the House of Commons is bred as a hound is bred to scent a fox. When English members are besieged in their 'surgeries', and threatened through their postbags with loss of votes and seats, if they persist in legislating for the Church of England, then, and only then, will they know that there is a 'demand'.

Bishops and functionaries of the General Synod are apt to be startled when they discover that Members of Parliament who concern themselves with the Church of England and with its legislation are almost invariably extremely conservative, not to say reactionary, quite irrespective of their party allegiance or their individual line of thinking on other matters. This ought to be a salutary observation. It ought to give food for thought if those whose business, nay, whose very existence, is bound up in keeping in touch with the grass roots in their constituencies, detecting 'the way the wind blows' and trimming their sails to it, turn out, where the Church of England, its law and worship and doctrine are concerned, to be totally unreconstructed and quite horribly allergic to what is fashionable or *avant garde* in the General Synod. It would be unwise to deduce that members are ignorant or unthinking. Are they not perhaps all too representative? Could it be Church House and not St Stephen's that is out of touch?

If Parliament remains the supreme legislature of the Church of England, it not merely will not but can not rubber stamp all and any measures submitted to it by the General Synod. There are those who believe that this proposition poses for the Synod a dilemma between confrontation with Parliament, leading to formal termination of the royal supremacy, or acquiescence in a subordinate and essentially advisory status, with no 'inherent authority of its own' (an expression used in the General Synod by the Bishop of Kensington). Quite apart from any question whether the confrontation would enjoy sufficient support among the Church's members and the public in general for it to succeed, I believe that, like most such stark dilemmas, this one is unreal.

Parliament is past master in the art of living with insoluble dilemmas: that is part of the political genius which has enabled the English people to create and maintain a parliamentary monarchy. Parliament, and the House of Commons in particular, has not the remotest intention of concerning itself, aye or no, with the overwhelming majority of changes in the law which the General Synod, using its far from over-hasty procedures, may find in the course of the years to be 'expedient' (blessed word). We have enough on our legislative plate not to want all that to be ladled on to it for the full treatment. On the other hand, there are some changes in the law of the Church of England which Parliament, and particularly what George II called 'that damned House of Commons', will not pass. What is necessary is that degree of mutual understanding between the two bodies which will ensure that both of them respect these facts. How is that common comprehension, that 'getting inside each other's mind', to be sufficiently achieved to avert collision?

The statutory machinery of the interlocking Legislative and Ecclesiastical Committees will not do the job. It is too formal and, without offence, too unpolitical. What is wanted must be both informal and political. Those who guide the General Synod must not be too proud to try to understand what makes Parliament 'tick' in ways that to them are disconcerting and disappointing. It would be worth the effort, and it would be welcomed in Westminster, where, if we hate anything, we hate *faits accomplis* and are practised in deftly avoiding them. That is why I have no intention of using this Chapter to set down specific proposals in black and white. There are precedents; and there are people of sufficient goodwill in Parliament and the General Synod to find a way of using them.

There is a third party to all this, however, and this Chapter would be incomplete if it were left out. The Crown is not only the Crown in Parliament: it is also the Crown in Council—the executive. The two must chime together. A recent leading article under the title 'Is Confrontation Coming?'[3] referred to 'the illusion that since the passing of the Worship and Doctrine Measure and the setting up of the Crown Appointments Commission the Church has the substance, if not the appearance, of power'. The collocation of the two items in that sentence is apt and significant. The executive functioning of the Crown on advice is no less integral to its governorship of the Church of England than is its legislative functioning by the advice and consent of Parliament. There is no doubt what the advice in question is. It is the collective advice, tendered on their behalf by the Prime Minister, of ministers who command the confidence of the House of Commons. On no other advice is the executive authority of the Crown exercised in this country, and on no other advice *can* it be exercised. So long therefore as the Church of England is governed on earth by the Crown of England, the Crown's executive acts as governor of the Church must be on the advice of ministers.

Such acts indisputably include the appointment of the prelates, no less than secular government includes appointments to the lay offices in the state. This logic in no way depends upon, or, still less, is invalidated by, the fact that diocesan bishops—since 1848 *certain* diocesan bishops only—have places in Parliament, the House of Lords, as a consequence of the feudal rights which were owed to the Crown by their predecessors in respect of the temporalities of their sees—in other words, as barons. If the prelatical office were confined to possession of the spiritualities, to the possession and exercise of episcopal functions in relation to the Church, appoint-

ment to that office by the Crown on the advice of ministers would
be no less implicit in the royal supremacy. Indeed, one of the
achievements of the Henrician Reformation settlement was the
final and logical termination which, so far as England was concerned, it brought to the ancient and, in papal terms, insoluble
investiture controversy by recombining temporal and ecclesiastical
sovereignty.

It is now nine years since an event occurred more blatantly
incompatible with the essential character of the Church of England
than any claim to effective power of legislation which might be
advanced or implied on behalf of the General Synod. In June 1976
Prime Minister Callaghan announced a proposal that in future the
Crown would not be advised to appoint to a bishopric any person
who was not one of two or more nominated for that purpose by a
body described as 'set up by the Church'. If anyone doubts that
this proposal, if it had any effect at all, would amount to annulment
of the royal supremacy, let it be considered what would be the
consequences of a comparable restriction in any other field of the
advice on which the Crown is constitutionally obliged to act.

The proposals were announced in a written answer to the then
Leader of the Opposition and purported to be 'supported by the
leaders of the main Opposition parties'. Staggeringly, no debate or
discussion of them whatsoever has taken place from that day to this
in either House of Parliament. Nevertheless they have been treated
as having come into effect as a result of a favourable vote in the
subsequent session of the General Synod. With breath-taking
effrontery Prime Minister Callaghan stated that 'arrangements on
these lines would not in themselves involve legislation'. Despite
the weasel words 'in themselves', a more insultingly preposterous
assertion could not have been advanced.

It amounted to asserting that the royal supremacy in the Church
of England, though by law established, can be repudiated and
rendered invalid by a simple statement on the part of the Prime
Minister and other politicians that in tendering advice to the
Crown on the appointment of bishops in the Church they would
limit themselves to persons nominated by an unspecified body in
an unspecified manner, so that in effect they themselves are not
responsible for that advice. That the law of the land can be thus
changed by prime ministerial declaration, because other party
leaders and the General Synod give assent to it, is not a proposition

which anyone concerned for the rights and liberties guaranteed to the people of this country by Parliament could for an instant accept.

It would in my opinion be erroneous to deduce from the mere silence of Parliament for the last eight years on the subject of the so-called concordat of 1976 that this will remain unbroken, and that the executive and legislative supremacy of the Crown in the Church of England can be evacuated of all reality by a series of wheezes which, in the words of Prime Minister Callaghan's Written Answer, will 'settle this issue in a satisfactory way for the foreseeable future'. If what the Answer called 'the Church'— which turns out to mean the pyramidal elective process embodied in the constitition of the General Synod—intends to 'have, and be seen to have, a greater say in the process of choosing its leaders', the removal of responsibility from ministers answerable to Parliament cannot be effected within a Church of England still by law established under the royal supremacy.

A church which 'chooses its leaders', like a church which 'makes its own laws', will not long remain the church which is the common right and possession of all the people of England. Whether the representatives of the people of England are prepared to see that possession and right removed from them, we have yet to learn. It would, however, in the matter of appointments as in that of legislation, be misunderstanding the attitude of Parliament to suppose that it wishes ministerial responsibility for advising the Crown on the executive exercise of the royal prerogative to be used in any way to the offence or scandal of the people of the Church of England.

The prominence of references to the Bishop of Durham in the debate of 15 July 1984, which ended in the House of Commons rejecting the Appointment of Bishops Measure, was neither adventitious nor a sign of levity. What the House was in effect saying was this: episcopal appointments made by the Crown on prime ministerial advice may from time to time have been open to criticism but we see no merit or advantage to the Church of England in destroying lay supremacy in order that something called 'the Church' can make appointments by which the Church itself is divided and scandalized.

Parliament knows very well that royal patronage exercised on political advice will often pass over the saintliest and the wisest. So will any other system of preferment to institutional office. What Parliament also knows, however, is that there is no substitute for the sanction of visible and personal political responsibility if the institution is to be a national, not a sectional possession.

NOTES

1 In recent years the case which caused most offence was the passage of the Worship and Doctrine Measure, 1974 by the 'payroll vote' against the manifest sense of the debate. The exception which proved the rule was the defeat of the Appointment of Bishops Measure on 15 July 1984 because of the Government's decision, which I elicited at the commencement of the debate, to stand aside.

2 Of 334 members of the October 1974 House of Commons who answered an inquiry on their religious belief, 203 reported 'Church of England' (*Cassell's Parliamentary Directory*).

3 *English Churchman* (10/17 May 1985).

9

Councils of Authority

Geoffrey Rowell

The General Synod of the Church of England, although only fifteen years old, was born out of a long process of development. Any assessment of the place of the Synod, its theological grounding and its limitations must take that development into account. It may be said to have two main aspects. One is the place given to conciliar authority within the Anglican theological tradition from the sixteenth century onwards. The other is the historical process which led more particularly to the establishment of synodical government and which has shaped and coloured the character of the Synod. Both of these themes must be related to that of a divided Church growing into unity. Synodical decisions are the decisions of a local council of the Church. They are partly decisions about government, finance and organization, which are domestic matters raising few questions beyond the ordering of the affairs of the Church of England, being simply the necessary concomitants of the working of any Church or institution. Other decisions are more far-reaching and raise questions which relate first to the Anglican Communion as a whole, and secondly to other Churches and traditions. There is a need to reflect much more explicitly on the relation of a local synod to the world-wide Church and to ask in respect of questions with this wider dimension how far the Synod has a *theological* authority rather than a legal one to act in these matters unilaterally. Even in our divided Church we recognize that we share much in common with Christians of other traditions—*that* for Anglicans, who have historically appealed to the witness of the Church of the early centuries as the touchstone of their faith is nothing new. The various contemporary dialogues between the Anglican Communion and other Churches only serve to underline this, witnessing to a shared Christian inheritance even in areas which were thought to divide which is both impressive and carries with it obligations of care for this common tradition.

Anglicans and Councils

The authority claimed by and accorded to the General Synod is a conciliar authority. Such authority has been accorded a high place in Anglican self-understanding, though distinctions have been properly and carefully drawn between General or Ecumenical Councils of the Church, and provincial or local councils. Article XXI of the Thirty-Nine Articles deals with General Councils. It follows the Article on the Authority of the Church, which states that the Church has 'power to decree Rites or Ceremonies and authority in Controversies of Faith' so long as these are in accord with Scripture. General Councils are stated to be subject to 'the commandment and will of Princes' for their calling. 'When they be gathered together ... they may err, and sometimes have erred, even in things pertaining unto God.' Their authority is expressly linked to that of Scripture. In Article XXXIV diversity of traditions and ceremonies is recognized and it is stated that 'every particular or national Church hath authority to ordain, change, and abolish, ceremonies or rites of the Church ordained only by man's authority, so that all things be done to edifying.'

Richard Hooker, in the *Laws of Ecclesiastical Polity*, acknowledged General Councils as expressions of the unity of the Church and the only means by which uniformity of rite and ceremony might be achieved.[1] The first four General Councils were, Hooker argued, binding on the Church of England, which nonetheless had authority to act as a province synodically.[2] In Hooker's understanding England was but one society, 'the Church and the Commonwealth'. 'Our estate is according to the pattern of God's ancient elect people, which people was not part of the commonwealth and part of them the Church of God, but the selfsame people whole and entire were both under one chief Governor, on whose supreme authority they did all depend.'[3] Just as the Catholic Philip II of Spain placed the kings of Israel and Judah on the façade of the Escorial to emphasize his role in a theocratic state, so Elizabethan Anglicanism was marked by a similar theocratic understanding.

Finding no precedent, except the Council of Jerusalem in Acts, for clergy alone constituting the conciliar authority of the national Church, Hooker argued for the place of Parliament as the lay synod of the Church, and for the royal supremacy, looking back

133

to the part played by Constantine and his successors in the early General Councils.[4] Such a theory, defending the Church of England against Puritan voluntarism on the one hand and the claims of the papacy on the other, reflected the Reformation period's concern with national Churches, the doctrine of the godly prince providing an alternative locus of authority to that of the see of Rome. Its basis was that of an establishment and a national Church. In its formative period Anglican understanding of councils and authority was shaped by the need to defend the autonomy of the national Church against the international claims of the papacy. That left Anglicans with a reference to the undivided church of antiquity, remote in time, but with a weak grasp of the *oikumene*. Like similar ecclesiologies on the Continent it was vulnerable both to the secularization of society and the reality of a world-wide Church. Moreover in Anglicanism, as in English society of which it was part, the constitution was to a large extent unwritten. That has many virtues, not least the avoidance of legalism and over-definition, but it also has limitations which perhaps become apparent when the Church needs to frame a common mind or articulate doctrine.

The seventeenth-century Anglican theologians defended with eloquence and learning the identity of Anglicanism with the faith of the early Church, revealed in the Scriptures and interpreted in the Creeds and the common witness of the Fathers. As Lancelot Andrewes put it: 'There is no principle dogma in which we do not agree with the Fathers and they with us.'[5] In mid-century Anglican apologetic came particularly under strain, when the victory of Cromwell in the Civil War overthrew the Church of England and drove many Anglicans into exile on the Continent. There they were faced with sharp challenges from Roman Catholics in particular. The defence of Anglicanism, although including the affirmation of the right of national Churches to order their affairs could not simply be left there. Hooker did not work well in a ghetto community in Paris. In writers like Herbert Thorndike and John Bramhall the authority of the early Church, expressed in the General Councils, was given a wider reference. The consensus of the Fathers as interpreters of Scripture and the traditions and practice of the early centuries were given an important place. Christianity, wrote Thorndike, consisted 'partly in matter of faith, partly in things to be done.'[6] Bramhall distinguished between *credenda* and *agenda*, both of which were the Anglican inheritance from the Church of the early centuries.[7] It was a distinction later to be employed by Newman in his differentiation of episcopal and prophetical tradition, the former being the creeds and definitions of councils and bishops, the latter being the worshipping context of faith and life out of which formal doctrinal definition arose as circumstances posed new questions and demanded explicit response.[8] The tradition of the early centuries was thus acknowledged as both explicit and implicit, formal statement and an inheritance of prayer and practice. Although Scripture remained the normative rule, the context in which Scripture was both received and interpreted was this larger tradition, both explicit and implicit. Acknowledging the authority of General Councils, Bramhall argued that they were 'extraordinary remedies, proper for curing or composing new differences of great concernment in Faith or discipline.' He cited medieval precedent for the Crown summoning synods in England, arguing against the monarchical pretensions of the papacy, though willingly recognizing the spiritual authority of the Bishop of Rome within the Western Church.[9] The Reformation was not the introduction of new doctrines, but the restoration of old and the repudiation of medieval accretions, whether such practices as indulgences, or the subtle elaborations of scholastic metaphysics, or a monarchical papacy.

The broad lines of Anglican apologetic in the seventeenth century stressed the continuity of the Church of England with the Church of the Fathers. Episcopacy was valued as embodying in a special way apostolic continuity and providing the external sign of the Church's unity, though not apart from 'the tradition of faith and the authority of the Scriptures which contain it.' As Thorndike put it, in the episcopate 'the Church . . . is a standing synod, able by consent of the chief Churches . . . to conclude the whole.'[10] The collegiality of the episcopate, and its corporate authority, is, by such writers at least, strongly affirmed.

Changing circumstances and Church polity

The theory that Parliament was the means by which the laity participated in the government of the Church of England was seriously called into question by the admission of non-Anglicans to

Parliament in the early nineteenth century, following the repeal of the Test and Corporation Acts and the passing of Catholic Emancipation. That change in the character of Parliament, combined with the subsequent threat of reforming legislation, was the circumstantial catalyst of the Oxford Movement. In part at least that Movement was a re-affirmation of Anglican identity in terms of continuity with the Church of the Fathers, the apostolic succession of the episcopate, and the spiritual and sacramental character of the Church. It was the Oxford Movement that provoked the pressure for the revival of Convocation, and it was men influenced by the Oxford Movement who sought appropriate expression for Anglican ecclesiology in the new colonial churches overseas. In New Zealand, where Bishop George Augustus Selwyn inaugurated a synod in 1859, one of his lay supporters commented:

> Of all religious denominations . . . the members of the Church of England are the most helpless when suddenly thrown upon their own resources in a new country . . . (They) find themselves in an anomalous position: they neither carry with them the ecclesiastical laws of their parent church, nor any authority to make new and more suitable laws for themselves.
>
> No measures having been taken by the parent church to provide her colonial branches with any system of local self-government, the bishops, clergy and laity of the Church of England in a British colony, instead of being a body 'fitly joined together by that which every joint supplieth', were a mere aggregation of disjointed members as powerless for many important purposes as an army without the Mutiny Act or Articles of War.[11]

Practical and theological considerations combined to promote the development of synodical forms of government in Anglican churches overseas. In a not dissimilar way the growth of these overseas churches led to pressure for conciliar meetings to express and affirm the common faith and discipline of the Anglican Communion, a term which came into use at the time of the SPG jubilee just over a decade before the first Lambeth Conference.[12] At that first conference Bishop Selwyn persuaded the conference to accept a resolution that 'unity of faith and discipline will be best maintained among the several branches of the Anglican Communion by due and canonical subordination of the synods of the several branches to the higher authority of a synod or synods above them.'[13] Selwyn perceived the need for a body which could give expression to the world Church and not just to local church requirements. The Lambeth Conferences have never functioned as such a formal synod as Selwyn envisaged, though it is note-worthy that both the Anglican Consultative Council and Primates' meetings have been established and grown in importance as part of the endeavour to preserve the unity of faith and discipline.

In England the ties of Church and State were such that rep-resentative church bodies evolved only gradually. Convocation was revived in 1852. The unofficial Church Congresses followed in 1861. There was pressure in some quarters for a General Assembly or Convention, and opposition to lay participation from High Churchmen such as Pusey, who feared that 'the admission of laity into synods' would invest 'them with an ecclesiatical office, which will develop itself sooner or later, I believe, to the destruction of the Faith.'[14] It was noted that the suppression of Convocation for a century and a half and the absence of lay assemblies had been in part responsible for the important place held by voluntary societies in providing meeting-places for Anglicans and opportunities for consultation at a national level.

It was the Enabling Act of 1919 which led to the setting up of the Church Assembly. Comment and discussion at that time reveal similar concerns to those currently met with in relation to the General Synod. The quasi-Parliamentary structure of the As-sembly was criticized both for fostering parties and for infringing the spiritual prerogatives of the Convocations. A committee in 1922 on the relations between Convocation and the National Assembly commented that 'on occasion the proceedings of the Assembly have appeared to trench upon the spiritual authority of the Convocations', warning that there was a danger 'not so much lest the National Assembly should assume supreme power in the affairs of the Church to the detriment of the spiritual authority of its synods as that such power should pass to it by default.'[15] High Churchmen drew distinctions between the authority of the As-sembly, based on representative principle, and the authority of Convocation derived 'from above'. There were other criticisms, of centralization, of remoteness from the parishes, of over-ruling of dioceses (countered by a reference to 'diocesanism' as 'the most virulent form of congregationalism') and of bureaucracy. There were numerous churchmen who believed that the only language and logic appropriate to church organizations were those which were personal and which employed traditional symbols. Committees and administration seemed to be part of an alien and fallen world. Defenders of the Church Assembly argued strongly for the need for efficiency, though they were aware of the double difficulty of being unable to fire the hearts of church people if they confined their deliberations to finance and organizational legislation and raising sharp questions about the locus of authority in the Church of England if they trespassed beyond it.

Dr Kenneth Thompson, who has studied the evolution of the Church Assembly from the perspective of a sociologist of religion, has argued that the basic division over the developing organization of central church government was 'between those who were concerned with instrumental adaptation, to enable the Church to go on fulfilling its responsibilities as an *ecclesia*, and, on the other hand, those who were concerned to stress the Church's autonomy as an institution, with its own distinct values.'[16] It was those who held to the latter position who 'looked beyond the *ecclesia* to the universal church for their principles, even though the practical consequence of this standpoint might reduce the Church of England to a less inclusive body.' This is a tension which still underlies debates about the authority and function of the General Synod. For some—or at least for some of the time—the Synod is, or should be, primarily a body concerned with necessary administration. When it considers wider questions, and particularly ones with a doctrinal reference, its parameters as a provincial synod must be defined in relation to a wider constituency. The character of that 'wider constituency' may be defined and valued in different ways. In some contexts it is the wider national community. In others it is the Anglican Communion. In yet others it is the Anglican Communion as sharing particular bonds with the Roman Catholic and Orthodox Churches, so that what is agreed in common by inheritance from the early Church cannot be altered unilaterally. Whatever criticisms may have been levelled against it the Tractarian 'branch theory' of the Church remains a powerful element in the ecclesiological consciousness of many Anglicans. There would be others, however, for whom the constituency of Evangelical Protestantism would be primary, and of them it might be said that their commitment to the Church of England is one of strategic adherence rather than ecclesiological principle.

In his study Dr Thompson saw the underlying tensions over the questions of authority in the Church as having led to an unsatisfactory compromise in the working of the Church Assembly. Not only was there the continuing factor of parliamentary control, there was also the separation of spiritual and non-spiritual matters. This was a necessary separation if support for the Assembly was to be forthcoming from Catholic Anglicans, but difficult to follow in practice. As Thompson comments, 'the acquiescence of the Catholic party had only been secured at the price of a compromise that denied the Church Assembly an unequivocal authority.'[17] Moreover, he continues:

> The parochial clergy were fearful that the Assembly would develop a bureaucratic organization which would rob them of their remaining independence and undermine their professional autonomy. Many of the measures passed by the Assembly in its early years seemed to bear hard on the clergy and a deep suspicion of the Assembly and its organization grew up. The result was that the clergy failed to provide the essential link in communicating information about the Assembly to the parochial level so as to develop an informed and sympathetic support for that body, and in consequence the Assembly was unable to bestow an unequivocal authority on its administrators and their activities.[18]

Synodical questions

When the General Synod succeeded the Church Assembly it inherited some of this traditional suspicion of the activities of a central bureaucratic organization. It also inherited unresolved questions about the locus of Anglican authority and the respective roles of the episcopate and the synod. With the House of Laity being brought more clearly into the processes of debate and decision-making there are further questions to be asked about the representative character of the laity who so participate. Even more than with the clergy, the selection of candidates, the extent of their theological awareness and the degree to which there can be a genuinely informed electorate, are questions which arise. There are further questions about the status of resolutions of the General

Synod. Insofar as these issue in practical legislation they are clearly put into effect, but there are questions concerning doctrine and the many matters which have doctrinal aspects which have not been satisfactorily resolved. Is a doctrinal decision of the General Synod an opinion or something binding on the Church? Questions also arise in relation to liturgical change. In a Church which has no confession of faith (in the sense that the continental Protestant churches are confessional churches) but which refers to the Book of Common Prayer as its doctrinal standard, what are the consequences of the promulgation of the Alternative Service Book for learning the mind of the Church, even though (both for party and parliamentary reasons) the Book of Common Prayer remains legally and historically a touchstone of Anglicanism? Does it matter that many Anglicans no longer use as a form of worship the book which has this status? If there were valid reasons for the process of liturgical revision does not this imply there were also shifts of emphasis, at the least, in Anglican understanding of worship and so of theology?

There is a further issue. Bodies such as the General Synod are law-making bodies. In the case of the General Synod its measures, if accepted by Parliament, become the law of the land. The formulations of law have a practical and organizational purpose, yet the equation of law and doctrine is dangerous. Anglicans, influenced in part by the perspective of the Greek Fathers, but also by an awareness of the dangers of elaborate systems of belief, have been reluctant definers. They have welcomed the idea of a hierarchy of truths, and have allowed a generous liberty in areas of Christian belief and practice that are not fundamental. There are, of course differences of opinion over what constitutes the fundamental core of the Christian tradition. Part of the dissatisfaction with the Synod in the Church belongs to disagreement over the status of particular beliefs and practices. Minimizers would exclude from the area of fundamentals, for example, the Virgin Birth (despite the credal affirmations) and also the traditional restriction of the ministerial priesthood to men. Others, holding that there is a wider area which belongs to the tradition, or from a proper caution or reverence in areas of uncertainty, would wish to include both. Again, there should be no dispute about the fact that the past inheritance of the Church *has* been culturally conditioned; but there is dispute about *what* is culturally conditioned and *how* that is to be sifted from what genuinely derives from the pattern of God's self-disclosure in Christ and his unfolding will for his people.

We need to articulate and define, yet we would do well to remember what Newman wrote on the fly-leaf of a copy of his *Development of Christian Doctrine*, 'Revelation is not of words.' As he told Pusey in 1867, 'we must ever hold ... that the object of faith is *not* simply certain articles, A.B.C.D. contained in dumb documents but the whole living word of God, explicit and implicit, as dispensed by His living Church.'[19] More recently the Dublin Statement of the Anglican-Orthodox dialogue is careful to begin by speaking of 'the mystery of the Church', reminding us that 'the mystery of the Church cannot be defined or fully described.' That statement then goes on to speak of the balance (if not the tension) between freedom and tradition, emphasizing that 'within the freedom existing in the Anglican Communion there is a commitment and responsibility to the tradition.' That tradition is dynamic and is to be seen operating particularly in 'the way in which the Church assimilates and sanctifies certain elements of the cultures of the various societies in which the Church lives'.[20] Fidelity to tradition is not a fossilizing bond but the living presence of the Holy Spirit in the Church. Contemporary councils and synods are therefore placed within the wider context of the life of the Church, and just as a council can only be recognized as ecumenical if it is received by the faithful (and here we might note the significance of the impact of the Second Vatican Council outside the Roman Catholic Church as a point of importance), so, it might be argued, a local council or synod can only be recognized as exercising binding authority if its actions are so approved and received both within its local area and within the communion of Churches within which it is placed.

Ecumenical context

The ecumenical context of synodical government puts particularly pertinent questions to synodical authority. In his Bampton Lectures for 1960 the present Bishop of Chichester wisely commented that 'the fragmentation of Christendom presents a major difficulty in the way of the application to modern times of principles drawn from Scripture and early tradition.'

It is reasonable to argue that no major innovation in doctrine ought to be made by a local and regional Church on its own authority. In a divided Christendom every part of the Church ought always to be conscious of its responsibility towards its separated brethren for what it does.

The acceptance of some such limitation upon freedom of action does not, however, involve the conclusion that nothing at all can be done, and a local Church must sometimes make decisions about matters of faith and worship. When that happens it is reasonable that the laity of the Church should exercise in respect of those decisions the functions which . . . belong to the laity as a whole.[21]

That is an appeal to the *consensus fidelium*.

It is easier to talk of the *consensus fidelium* than to devise means of ascertaining it. As it has been put by another writer, 'Anglicans are good at seeking the common mind, but not so good at enunciating it.'[22] This is true not simply as regards the place of laity in doctrinal affirmation, but also in relation to the role of bishops and clergy. There is more to an affirmation of faith than a synodical vote, though synodical votes are not irrelevant to the articulation of corporate faith. At the present time there is wide interest in the idea of 'reception' with regard to ecumenical texts, such as BEM and ARCIC, and it is noteworthy that the Faith and Order Advisory Group of the General Synod Board for Mission and Unity underlined the fact 'that the general acknowledgement of the ancient ecumenical councils to which Rome and the West assented was not immediate and in some cases took considerable time.' 'In other words, reception by the faithful is a continuing process of assimilation which is also a critical appropriation and interpretation.'[23] For an issue to come before Synod indicates a concern among the faithful; for an issue to be approved by Synod is not equivalent to the consent of the faithful. We need to find ways of expressing the relation of synodical decisions to the life of the Church as a whole, both Anglican and ecumenical, both in relation to England and to the world. As Richard Harries has warned, 'it would be fatal at this time . . . for the Church of England to order its affairs as though it intended to remain a separated body. Its future lies within the Catholic Church as a whole.'[24]

Questions concerning the character of and the constraints upon the synodical expression of authority within the Church of England raise fundamental ecclesiological issues to which other Churches are not strangers. The Anglican-Roman Catholic dialogue in particular has brought to the fore the difficult questions about how the mind of the Church is known and articulated, initiating with reference to the papacy questions about the nature and function of primacy in the Christian Church. The parliamentary model of the General Synod may well be a distorting mirror in seeking to answer some of these questions, for it needs a more explicit link with the worshipping life of the Church and a clearer articulation of the relation between synodical and episcopal authority. In an article on the context of faith and theology Professor Henry Chadwick has drawn out the conciliar sense of the early Church and its link with a doctrine of reception by the believing community, a process in which the leaders of that community have a particular part to play.

> The synodical gathering of bishops representing their local dioceses derives its authority from the body or bodies that have a stake in its deliberations and decisions. The wisdom of many is in general better than that of one, but only the assistance of the Holy Spirit can make a council, or any other human agency, secure against error. Early Christian councils met with the presence of Christ symbolized by the open Gospel and with the prayerful confidence that the Spirit would surely lead his Church into truth in those many matters where Scripture gave no guidance. The Lord had promised his presence where two or three were gathered in his name. The ancient Church did not understand this to mean that two or three bishops could be infallible. The moral unanimity of a council of many bishops has always been understood to have decision-making and binding force for the community represented. The Spirit gives the spiritual gift of discernment and spiritual judgment to baptized believers as well as to the commissioned teachers of the Church. The consensus of bishops in council is therefore integrally linked to the wider, universal consensus of the faithful, both clerical and lay; and that wider consensus has often exercised, gradually but decisively, a controlling critical interpretation of the decrees and definitions of even general councils. The reception of the believing community is integral to the process of

authoritative doctrinal or ethical decisions. In this process of reception the assent of major Christian leaders, patriarchs and metropolitans, and the pope himself, is an evident and practical necessity. The binding force of a definition is determined, however, not by a single bishop but by the agreement of all the bishops representing the universal church.[25]

As Thorndike had put it in the seventeenth century, in the episcopate 'the church is a standing synod able by consent of the chief Churches . . . to conclude the whole,' but only, we might add, insofar as that conclusion is received by the whole body of believers, a process which may well demand a long period of assimilation and assessment.

The sixteenth century, characterized by the emergence of European nation-states, left its mark on national Churches, and certainly on the Church of England. Claiming to be the Catholic Church in England, Reformed indeed but professing only the scriptural faith of the undivided Church, whose conciliar Creeds and doctrinal decisions and whose patterns of liturgy and order had a special authority, the marks of Tudor monarchy were left on it. The growth of the Anglican Communion and the process of ecumenical dialogue has placed question marks against some aspects of that inheritance. Narrow nationalism can no longer be a sufficient argument for standing alone, nor for a theology of synodical decision which leaves unanswered not only questions about the character and status of such decisions but the extent to which a Church is free to take unilateral decisions on that which is held in common. As Christian divisions are healed the imperatives of unity become more extensive and constraining. We need not only a more adequate theology of synodical government, but an ecclesiology which sets it clearly in the context of the organic unity of the Church, and of an understanding of tradition which sees it not as an inert inheritance from the past, but as 'the living force and inexhaustible source of 'the Church's "mission to the world",,' the 'unceasing presence of the revelation of the Word of God through the Holy Spirit.'[26]

NOTES

1 Hooker, Richard, *Laws of Ecclesiastical Polity*, I.x.14; IV.xiii.8.
2 ibid., VIII.ii.17; VII.viii.12.

3 ibid., VIII.i.7.

4 ibid., VIII.vi.7; v.2.

5 cited in McAdoo, H. R., *The Spirit of Anglicanism: A Survey of Anglican Theological Method in the Seventeenth Century* (London 1965), p.345.

6 Thorndike, H., *Works* (Library of Anglo-Catholic Theology (LACT) 1842–5), II, p.117 (*Principles of Christian Truth*, 1659).

7 Bramhall, J., *Works* (LACT, 1842), pp.470–1 (*Schism Guarded*, 1658).

8 Newman, J. H., *Lectures on the Prophetical Office of the Church*, 1837.

9 Bramhall, J., *Works*, II, pp. 307, 486, 547.

10 Tavard, G. H., *The Quest for Catholicity: a Study in Anglicanism* (London 1963); Thorndike, H., op.cit., II, p.117.

11 Tucker, H. W., *Memoir of the Life and Episcopate of George Augustus Selwyn, D.D.* (London 1900³), II, p.86.

12 Stephenson, Alan M. G., *Anglicanism and the Lambeth Conferences* (London 1978), p.16.

13 ibid., p.38.

14 q. Thompson, K. A., *Bureaucracy and Church Reform: The Organizational Response of the Church of England to Social Change 1800–1965* (Oxford 1970), p.100.

15 q. ibid., pp.84, 85.

16 ibid. p.219.

17 ibid. p.226.

18 ibid. p.242.

19 q. Goulder, M. D., ed., *Infallibility in the Church: An Anglican-Catholic Dialogue* (London 1968), p.79.

20 *Anglican-Orthodox Dialogue: The Dublin Agreed Statement 1984* (London 1984), pp.9, 29.

21 Kemp, E. W., *Counsel and Consent: Aspects of the Government of the Church as Exemplified in the History of the English Provincial Synods* (London 1961), p. 215.

22 Dudley, Martin, 'Waiting on the Common Mind: Authority in Anglicanism', in *One in Christ* (1984), p.75.

23 *Towards a Church of England Response to BEM and ARCIC* (GS 661) (London 1985), p.88.

24 Harries, Richard, *The Authority of Divine Love* (Oxford 1983), p.107.

25 in Vogel, A. A., ed., *Theology in Anglicanism* (Wilton, Connecticut 1984), p.26.

26 *Anglican-Orthodox Dialogue: The Dublin Agreed Statement*, pp.29–30.